DATE DUE

			PRINTED IN U.S.A.

THE HUMOUR OF SAMUEL BECKETT

The Humour of Samuel Beckett

Valerie Topsfield

St. Martin's Press   New York

First published in the United States of America in 1988

Printed in Hong Kong

ISBN 0–312–01571–2

Library of Congress Cataloging-in-Publication Data
Topsfield, Valerie.
The humour of Samuel Beckett/by Valerie Topsfield.
p.   cm.
Bibliography: p.
Includes index.
ISBN 0–312–01571–2: $29.95
1. Beckett, Samuel, 1906–   —Humor, satire, etc.   2. Comic, The,
in literature.   I. Title
PR6003.E282Z855 1988
848'.91409—dc19   87–30405
                                                                CIP

To Leslie

Contents

Acknowledgements

With thanks to Judith Slater, Brian Stone, Arnold Kettle, Graham Martin, John Fletcher, and to Samuel Beckett for permission to quote from an unpublished work (*Eleuthéria*).

VALERIE TOPSFIELD

because it is a pensum, or task, not a punishment; so that if the task is completed, there is a positive result.

He says, 'There is a continuous purgatorial process at work, in the sense that a vicious circle of humanity is being achieved, and this achievement depends on the recurrent predomination of one of two broad qualities.' (*Our Exagmination*, p. 22) These two broad qualities are of course 'good' and 'evil', and it is the individual's reaction to them, and choice between them, which produces results. As Beckett goes on to say, without resistance there is no eruption, and nothing comes of it. It is during our purgatory, here and now, that we have the power, thinks Beckett, to make this choice. In Hell and Paradise, Beckett says, there are no eruptions. It is only in purgatory that the conflict between good and evil produces the eruptions which enable 'the kitten to catch its tail'. And who are the agents of such eruptions? he asks, and answers, 'The partially purged'.

So it was as 'the partially purged' that Beckett began his six decades of writing. His motivation was twofold. He accepted it as a pensum, and he wanted to explore his own identity, a process begun in childhood and recalled throughout the works. Childhood is 'when you started not knowing who you were from Adam . . . no notion who it was saying what you were saying', 'making it up on the doorstep as you went along, making yourself all up again for the millionth time' (*That Time*, pp. 12 and 15). Sometimes the child has a multiple personality; in *Endgame* (p. 45) he speaks of 'the solitary child who turns himself into children, two, three, so as to be together, and whisper together in the dark'. The old man who was that child is still there in his latest works; in *Company* (1981), making stories about himself in the dark. In *Ill Seen, Ill Said* (1982) an old woman reminisces in the same fashion. In *Rockabye* (1982) another old woman rocks herself (like Murphy) into oblivion, as she recalls the past. The characters are strongly identified with the author, throughout the works.

This quest for identity is often discouraging, yet always worthwhile. When Watt grows tired of the search, the author enquires tartly: 'What had he learned? Nothing', but at least he saw himself clearer, 'was not that something? As the comparative is something. Whether more than its positive or less, whether less than its superlative or more . . .' (*Watt*, p. 147). The writer discovers himself, and a philosophy, through his characters, rather as he suspects God discovers himself through his creatures.

He charts this development with care, 'making the tot'. At the end of youth he notes that he is 'Good as gold now in the prime after a brief prodigality, Yea and suave, Suave, urbane, beyond good and evil' (*Sanies* 2, *Collected Poems*, p. 19). One of his most interesting creations, Moran, says that 'in spite of the deep lesions and wounds of the journey', he not only knew who he was but had a sharper and clearer sense of his identity than ever before (*Molloy*, p. 182). More immediately, as an author, the Unnamable confesses that his creatures have brought him some comfort: 'Under the skies, on the roads, in the towns, in the woods, in the hills, in the plains, by the shores, on the seas, behind my mannikins, I was not always sad . . .' (p. 22). The act of writing produced for him, as for Beckett, a satisfaction that life could not give.

Beckett thinks that our existential anxiety comes from a sense of impermanence, which is frustrating: 'The mortal microcosm cannot forgive the relative immortality of the macrocosm' (*Proust*, p. 21) but, borrowing from Bruno, he offers consolation. We are all parts of a greater whole: 'the individual and the universal cannot be considered as distinct from each other' (*Our Exagmination*, p. 7), and there is a kind of survival for us in our works: 'The lamp is more important than the lamplighter' (*Our Exagmination*, p. 7). Moran echoes this thought more explicitly during his search for Molloy (his *alter ego*): 'what I was doing I was doing neither for Molloy, who mattered nothing to me, nor for myself, of whom I despaired, but on behalf of a cause which, while having need of us to be accomplished, was in its essence anonymous, and would subsist, haunting the minds of men, when its miserable artisans should be no more' (*Molloy*, p. 123). To write, then, is imperative, even though there is 'little to write about', excepting 'This ballsaching poppycock about life and death, if that's what it is all about, and I suppose it is, for nothing was ever about anything else to the best of my recollection . . .' (*Malone Dies*, p. 53). In a letter to George Reavey (18 December 1971), Beckett wrote: 'I could not have gone through the awful wretchedness of life without having left a stain upon the silence.' Writing has given Beckett, in an image of the oyster, 'a little pearl of forlorn solace' (*How It Is*, p. 48), and he has achieved, what he wanted from the start, communication with his reader; real, however tenuous: 'The experience of my reader shall be between the phrases, in the silence . . . his experience shall be the menace, the miracle, the memory of unspeakable trajectory' (*Dream of Fair to Middling Women*, p. 123).

Beckett's inspiration on the long journey has always been nature, which evokes his most positive statements. His appreciation of her powers is constant. The sky, stars, sea, sun, are all used as images of what is strongest, clearest, most inspiring in the hotchpotch of existence, and what is best in us. Moran says: 'I give thanks for evening that brings out the lights, the stars in the sky, and on earth the brave little lights of men' (*Molloy*, p. 171). His love of natural things is sensuous; about the sky, he says: 'Most of the time it was a mixture of white, blue and grey, and then at evening all the evening colours. I felt it weighing softly on my face, I rubbed my face against it, one cheek after the other, turning my head from side to side' ('The End', *Four Novellas*, p. 87). Hamm's last dream, in *Endgame*, is of sleep, in which he might make love, see woods, sky, earth (p. 19). Water, like life, ever in flux, is a favourite image. The character in *First Love* admires 'in spite of the dark, in spite of my fluster, the way still or scarcely flowing water reaches up, as though athirst, to that falling from the sky' (*First Love*, p. 43). Winter, hard on one who is homeless, is still a source of inspiration, 'One should not dread the winter, it too has its bounties, the snow gives warmth and deadens the tumult, and its pale days are soon over' (*First Love*, p. 60), and summer, evanescent as it is, is an image of something which has lasting value. Arsene, in *Watt* (p. 54) says: 'When I lie dying, Mr Watt, behind the red screen, you know, perhaps that is the word that will sound, summer, and the words for summer things. Not that I ever cared much for them. But some call for the priest, and others for the long days when the sun was a burden.' Because nature caters for all tastes, there is something for everyone: 'Sam likes the sun, Watt the wind. For when on Sam the sun shone bright, then in a vacuum panted Watt, and when Watt like a leaf was tossed, then stumbled Sam in deepest night. But ah, when exceptionally the desired degrees of ventilation and radiance were united, in the little garden, then we were peers in peace, each in his own way, until the wind fell, the sun declined' (*Watt*, p. 151). After a long parting, nature shares in their reunion and rejoices: 'To be together again after so long, who love the sunny wind, the windy sun, in the sun, in the wind, that is perhaps something, perhaps something' (p. 162). Beckett's love of the earth has a positive, calming effect, and he parodies the scriptures: 'It was always from the earth, rather than from the sky, notwithstanding its reputation, that my help came in time of trouble' ('The Calmative', *Four Novellas*, p. 56).

Beckett's other aid, in the long journey, has been his perception, in life's contrasts, of the advantage of an empirical approach. This is expressed humorously in *More Pricks than Kicks*, in the cheering and realistic dictum: 'Hope for the best and expect the worst', and is developed, in *Mercier and Camier* (p. 7), when they consult together before embarking on their quest, 'weighing with all the calm at their command what benefits they might hope from it, what ills apprehend, maintaining turn about the dark side and the rosy'. This appreciation of the conflicts and contrasts in any undertaking, and especially in the journey of existence, is described by Mercier as 'a sense of proportion', when he tells Camier, who has no sense of proportion: 'When you fear for your cyst, think of your fistula. And when you tremble for your fistula consider your chancre. This method holds equally for what is called happiness' (p. 58). The same 'sense of proportion' is later referred to, in *Waiting for Godot*, in the quotation: 'Hope deferred maketh the heart sick . . .'. Beckett has said that it is the second part of the verse, not quoted, which is important: 'but when the desire cometh, it is a tree of life'.

Beckett's method is allusive, based on poetry, which alone can hope to express the inexpressible. As a poet, he believes that poetry underlies all creative works: 'Poetry is the foundation of writing' (*Our Exagmination*, p. 11), and 'all poetry as discriminated from the various paradigms of prosody is prayer' (*Dublin Magazine* IX, 1934, p. 8). Beckett sees poetry as the prime factor in philosophy because it is not purely intellectual but is 'all passion and feeling, and animates the inanimate' (*Our Exagmination*, p. 10), and he quotes the Scholastics' axiom: 'Niente è nell' intelleto che prima non sia nel senso'. Characteristically, and self mockingly he later puts this into the screech of the parrot, in *Murphy*, who will repeat the first part only, in Latin: '*nihil in intellectu*', nothing in the intellect, and refuses to finish the quotation. In his writings, Beckett has contrived to appeal to the latent sensibility and intelligence of humanity and, although the impermanence and uncertainty of existence engage the attack of his scathing wit and ribaldry, there are allusions throughout the works to some lasting verities.

For example, Murphy, emerging from unconsciousness, after

an accident with his rocking chair, finds such reassurance at the sight of Celia: 'The beloved features emerging from chaos were the face against the big blooming buzzing confusion of his world' (p. 21). In *First Love*, the father's face on his death bolster had seemed 'to hint at some form of aesthetics relevant to man' (p. 3). Arsene, in *Watt*, refers to a certainty beyond our uncertainties when he says that behind the shadows of existence, 'our arrival in the world and gradual fading out of it', lies 'the shadow of purpose, of the purpose that budding withers, that withering buds, whose blooming is a budding withering' (p. 57). This process is alluded to in *Endgame*, in the phrase: 'Something is taking its course.' There is more to existence, Beckett tells us, than meets the eye – like Mercier's arctic flowers, which last half an hour (p. 118), (the 'fleurs arctiques' of Enueg 1), which Camier cannot see:

> Is that your flowers? said Camier.
> Did you see? said Mercier.
> I saw a few pale gleams, said Camier.
> You need to have the knack, said Mercier.   (p. 121)

When Camier asks if there will ever be order, Mercier replies: 'Yes I believe, not firmly, no, but I believe, yes, the day is coming when all will be in order at last.' Camier cries: 'That will be delightful', and the sceptical Mercier answers, 'Let us hope so' (p. 18). Mercier is painfully aware of the contradictions of existence, its absurdities, and, on the other hand, its positive aspects. 'All is *vox inanis*', he announces, 'save certain days, certain conjurations' (p. 84).

Fourteen years later, in *How It Is*, a continued 'deterioration of the sense of humour' is noted, 'fewer tears too that too they are failing too' (p. 20). At last the stage has been reached of acceptance of the way things are. The conflict between 'tears and laughter' is resolved, but the battle with language goes on. There are still reminders of the 'certain days, certain conjurations' when the *vox inanis* is less insistent, and this, too, is a continuing process. Twenty years after the summing up of *How It Is*, in his latest works, Beckett's now aging and dying character is still feeling his way, still not certain that existence is in vain. The last moments hold 'some promise yet of grace to be savoured' and, like Hamm, the character is loath to take a final bow: 'No. One moment more.

One last. Grace to breathe that void. Know happiness.' The waiting continues. *How It Is*, Beckett says, is 'the end of laughter and tears', but there is still a humorous appreciation of the contrasts, 'the dark side and the rosy', of existence; and, most important, the endeavour must continue to 'utter or eff the ineffable'.

1

Beckett's Literary Antecedents and Some Philosophers

A broad view of the literary and philosophical background to his writings helps to illuminate Beckett's gloomy, humorous view of man's place in the universe. Part of his comic method is his borrowing from, or misquotation of the works of others. He is quite open in his borrowings, and has said that he has no objection to being likened to other writers. (But in the Addenda to *Watt* there is a curse on 'those who have said what we want to say': pereant qui ante nos nostra dixerunt.) Criticism of the status quo, and its transformation into fantasy is a universal genre, not special to any period, and it is interesting to trace Beckettian echoes in the questioning by earlier writers of 'the issueless predicament of existence'.

Several of his critics have agreed that Beckett is working within the traditions of Dante, Swift or Sterne. Vivian Mercier has drawn attention to the Anglo-Irish irreverence in the tradition of Swift.[1] 'The spirit in which he writes', said Edwin Muir, 'is rather that of Sterne, and he reduces everything, or raises it, as the case may be, to intellectual fantasy.[2] Christopher Ricks speaks of Beckett's debt to Dante and Swift, which 'shows him as less perversely gloomy than appears at first sight'.[3] John Fletcher says that 'in common with Voltaire he is the master of the emotionally neutral remark that serves to highlight the cruel or ridiculous aspect which the author, behind his mask, wishes to castigate'.[4]

Beckett's earliest and most profound influence was Dante, from whom he drew the prototype of his ineffective heroes, the indolent Belacqua, like himself, a student of Italian. Dante's *Purgatorio* is a journey in limbo; man is seen pitiably struggling in the mud. But beyond the pity there is a calm detachment, and a perception that, underlying the human experience of suffering and joy, there is order and purpose. It also affirms that man is not

9

only a collection of decaying cells, and can rise above a bleak existence, in which suffering may be a catalyst. Beckett, in *More Pricks than Kicks* (p. 18), has Belacqua pondering on Dante's pun: 'qui vive la pieta quando e ben morta . . .', and wondering 'why not piety and pity both, even down below?' (p. 20). Thirty years on, in *How It Is*, he refers again to Dante, the 'human voice there within an inch or two of my dream', adding, 'if I have to learn Italian obviously it will be less amusing'. Acknowledging his debt to Dante, he says: 'oriented as he is he must have been following the same road as I before he dropped' (p. 63). Beckett's concern is not hell or heaven, but the purgatory which may be productive.

Purgatory is for Beckett 'a flood of movement and vitality', more productive than 'the static lifelessness of unrelieved viciousness' of Hell, or 'the static lifelessness of unrelieved immaculation' of Paradise (*Our Exagmination*, p. 22); and in *Proust*, written in 1931, Beckett sees suffering as leading to artistic creation. 'Suffering', says Beckett, speaking of Proust, 'opens a window on the real and is the main condition of the artistic experience', and art is the 'one ideal and inviolable element in a corruptible world' (p. 28). Beckett's heroes compensate for the misery of existence by making up stories, and save themselves from extinction through memory. This recapturing of experience is a series of paradoxes, which Beckett describes in *Proust* as being 'the real without being merely actual, ideal without being merely abstract, the ideal real, the essential, the extra-temporal' (p. 75). Memory is 'a clinical laboratory, stocked with poison and remedy, stimulant and sedative', and time is 'creative and destructive' (p. 78). He sees it as the element in which Proust discovers himself as an artist, and admires him for his victory over time and therefore over death (p. 69). Art is for Beckett, as for Proust, the main reason for, and proof of his existence, and a means of making personal death irrelevant. They live in a world of metaphors and Beckett says, referring to Proust's world, that 'it is expressed metaphorically . . . because it is apprehended metaphorically' (*Proust*, 88).

The urge to escape the tyranny of linear time, which began in the novel with Sterne, is a concept which preoccupies many twentieth-century writers. The comedy of Sterne and Beckett is a mask for their sensibility, and they play the clown. In his dedication of *Tristram Shandy*, Sterne says he jests 'in a constant endeavour to fence against the infinities of ill-health, and the evils

of life, by mirth'. Like Beckett, he is incensed by the apparent lack
of reason and justice of the universe. Despite this, Sterne believes
in a benevolent deity; Beckett is not certain about this, but agrees
that man is not perfectible, and takes refuge in laughter. Although
Beckett and Sterne are capable of satire, their dispositions incline
them to temper its sting, and to show a tolerance denied to the
angry satirist. Sterne points out that 'There is a difference between
Bitterness and Saltness, that is, – between the malignity and the
festivity of wit, – the one is a mere quickness of apprehension,
void of humanity – . . . the other willingly hurts no man but
give[s] a new colour to absurdity'.

Several critics have seen similarities between Beckett and Swift,
who wrote in a letter to Pope in 1725: 'The chief end I propose to
myself in all my labours is to vex the world rather than divert it'.
Beckett, too, stirs up as much as he entertains. Beckett and Swift
recognise the power of laughter to hold the attention of the
audience, as Swift said in 'Epistle to a Lady' (*Poems*, II):

> I may storm and rage in vain;
> It but stupefies your Brain.
> But with Raillery to nettle,
> Set your Thoughts upon their Mettle:
> Gives Imagination scope . . . .

Beckett introduced clowning, for instance the trouser-dropping in
Waiting for Godot, for the same reason.

Beckett and Swift see man's chief conflict in the contradictions
of flesh and spirit, particularly the 'love of life' which, without a
body, the mind could reject. This love of life, Swift says, (*Works*,
III, p. 309) but for the lusts of the flesh, 'from the dictates of
reason, every man would despise and wish at an end, or that it
never had a beginning', and Beckett's Murphy, too, wishes he
could 'live inside his head' (*Murphy*, p. 131), and not be distracted
by his passion for Celia and ginger biscuits.

Beckett shares with Swift a taste for the grotesque in wit,
imagery and wordplay; they push their ideas to the point of
absurdity, which has the effect of shocking the reader into
laughter. Swift argues in *A Modest Proposal* that overbreeding in
Ireland could be helped by eating surplus children. The incongruity
of the notion and reasonable tone have a comic effect. The
grotesque, as a clash of opposite emotions, is an appropriate form

of expression of the problematical nature of existence now, as then, and has been taken over by Beckett, Ionesco and Pinter in our own age. Beckett's description of the Lynch family in *Watt* is in this tradition. All thirteen of them are repellent and diseased but his attitude is ambivalent, and his tone is comic: 'Then there was Joe's boy Tom, aged 41 years, unfortunately subject alternately to fits of exaltation which rendered him incapable of the least exertion, and of depression, during which he could stir neither hand nor foot.' This tragi-comic attitude, expressed grotesquely, continues throughout the novels and plays. Beckett also shares with Swift a distrust of life. Swift thought 'God did not intend life to be a blessing' (*Journal to Stella*, 3 January 1723 in *Works*, II, p. 410), and from an early age took as his motto the passage of Job beginning 'Let the day perish wherein I was born, and the night in which it was said, There is a man child conceived.' Beckett, whose characters often wish they had never left the womb, also quotes this passage in *Murphy*.

Swift and Beckett are deeply ironical, but use irony in different ways, Swift to dissociate himself from the intensity of his rage; Beckett to distance himself from what he finds too painful. As a satirist, Swift would have liked to change things: 'I have finished my *Travels*', he wrote, 'and am now transcribing them. They are admirable things and will wonderfully mend the World.' He was driven by savage anger (*saeva indignatio*), as he said in his own epitaph. Living in an age of Reason, he was bitterly disillusioned by the irrationality of humankind. In such an age his disenchantment was more bitter than that of Beckett who, in an age of disintegration of religion and ethics, decided early in life that the shortcomings of man are ludicrous and inspire savage humour rather than savage rage. It is in his distanced approach that Beckett differs from the involved and angry Swift.

'The folly of human wishes has always been a standing object of mirth and declamation and has been ridiculed and lamented from age to age . . . .' So wrote Samuel Johnson (in *Rambler*), a writer admired by Beckett, who shares his distaste of human complacency and pretensions, and on whose life he based a play, *Human Wishes*, never finished, but its dialogue prefigures that of *Waiting for Godot*. The black comedy of the later maimed heroes is first expressed by Mrs Williams in *Human Wishes*, 'I may be old, I may be blind, halt and maim, I may be dying of a pituitous defluxion, but my hearing is unimpaired.'

It is the unevenness of fortune which inspires Johnson's bitter humour, neither tragedy nor comedy but a defiant tragi-comedy. Johnson blames life's uncertainty on 'frolic beings' who 'take a man in the midst of his business or pleasure and knock him down with an apoplexy', whose sport it is 'to see a man tumble with an epilepsy, and revive and tumble again, and all this he knows not why' (*Works*, VI, pp. 64–5). Such a man is the ancestor of Beckett's heroes. Johnson believes that man can grapple with misfortune: 'To strive with difficulties and to conquer them is the highest human felicity; the next is to strive and deserve to conquer', he wrote (*Adventurer*, III), and Beckett says of his own hero, Murphy, that although his other characters 'whinge sooner or later', Murphy, *who is not a puppet*, never whinges (*Murphy*, p. 86). He has accepted that that is the way things are, and no amount of whinging will change it; for Murphy, life *is* tragi-comic. Dr Johnson, as a critic of the plays of Shakespeare which express this notion, says the plays are 'not in the rigorous and critical sense either tragedies or comedies, but compositions of a distinct kind: exhibiting the real state of sublunary nature, which partakes of good and evil, joy and sorrow, mingled with endless variety of proportion and innumerable modes of combination; and expressing the course of the world; in which the loss of one is the gain of another; in which at the same time, the reveller is hasting to his wine, and the mourner is burying his friend; in which the malignity of one is sometimes defeated by the frolick of another; and many mischiefs and many benefits are done and hindered without design'.[5] These are the paradoxes which Beckett is trying to express; in other words, 'how it is'.

The uncertainty and seeming lack of design of existence is strikingly expressed in the same image by both writers; by Beckett in a fragment of Hölderlin's poem which appears as an Addendum in *Watt*, and by Johnson in 'The Vanity of Human Wishes'. The text of Hölderlin's Hyperion reads:

> But to us it is given
> Nowhere to rest,
> Suffering men
> Falter and fall
> Blindly from one
> Hour to the next
> Like water flung down

> From cliff to cliff,
> Yearlong into uncertainty.
> ('Hyperion')

In 'The Vanity of Human Wishes' Johnson uses the same image of man being tumbled like water, with no say in his destiny:

> Must helpless man, in ignorance sedate,
> Roll darkling down the torrent of his fate?

The same thought, and the same image for it, has struck all three: Johnson, Hölderlin and Beckett. Johnson queries fate, but the two later writers accept it more stoically.

Beckett is alive not only to the qualities of writers of the past but also to those of his contemporaries whose focus is the same aspect of existence. He called Céline's *Voyage au bout de la nuit* (1932) 'the greatest novel in English or French'.[6] Like Beckett's, Céline's works are basically autobiographical; personal experiences go to make their *louche* heroes, and writing is an exorcism. Céline, a doctor, was sickened by the diseased humanity which moved 'like a waterfall' in front of his spectacles, 'for 30 years morning, noon and night'.[7] Yet, like Beckett, he empathises with the underdog and hates bourgeois complacency. Both see life as a journey, like Dante's Virgil's, through purgatory.

In *Voyage au bout de la nuit*, Céline's Bardamu is a Beckettian figure, apathetic, maimed, shabby and frustrated. Things fade, abandon him and die, yet he is impelled onward: 'To feel grief isn't all, one must be able to start the music all over again, to go on to look for more grief . . . bear even more' (p. 489), a thought which echoes in the final words of the Unnamable. Like Murphy, Bardamu meets a good-hearted prostitute (*Voyage*, p. 227) who, like Beckett's Celia, symbolises kindness and devotion, evoking genuine feeling in Bardamu, as Celia does in Murphy. Bardamu, like Murphy, is an attendant in an asylum, which is seen as a shelter from a cruel society. In an interview, Céline said: 'The world of the asylum forms a sort of insulating layer. It's perfect . . .',[8] and Murphy shares this opinion, envying Beckett's lunatics who have escaped the world in the Magdalen Mercy Seat.

Beckett and Céline are obsessed by the theme of the inhumanity of man to man. Céline explains why he writes as he does: 'For me, real objective life is impossible, *unbearable* . . . . So I transpose as I go along, without breaking my stride. I suppose it's more or less the world's pervasive illness we call poetry.'[9] Art, fantasy, dream and myth are the antidotes such writers adopt against the poison of the world. What is central in Céline and Beckett is this sense of poetry. Painstaking craftsmen, they write and rewrite, using unconventional language and forms, trying to say it as it is. Céline said: 'I start every sentence ten or twenty times . . . it's all measured to the millimetre.' Beckett shares his care and regard for language.

It is this task which makes existence bearable. In a letter, Céline said: 'I am nothing more than an instrument of work . . . . Existence is much too heavy and monotonous to bear without constant artifice.'[10] Beckett also takes the view that putting one's experience into words may be a release from fears and anxiety. Céline says: 'We'll only have some peace once everything has been said, once and for all, then one will finally be able to keep still and be no longer afraid to keep one's mouth shut' (*Voyage*, p. 323). This thought is echoed by the Unnamable: 'Perhaps I've said the thing that had to be said that gives me the right to be done with speech.'

The wretchedness and absurdities of life, which they are compelled to record, sometimes in brutal language and obscenities to express their pain, gives these two writers much in common. Ruby Cohn has pointed out the influence of Céline's ideas and colloquial style on Beckett's *Trilogy* in French and quotes a passage from *Voyage au bout de la nuit* which illustrates this: 'Quand on sera au bord du trou, faudra pas faire les malins nous autres, mais faudra pas oublier non plus, faudra raconter tout sans changer un mot, de ce qu'on a vu de plus vicieux chez les hommes, et puis poser sa chique et puis déscendre. Ça suffit comme boulot pour une vie toute entière.'[11] The rhythms, turn of phrase, and theme, have a Beckettian tone, but the emphasis is different, for Beckett is concerned, not so much with the vicious, as with the victimised, and is more resigned than Céline, and more humorous.

From the point of view of humour, whether black and bizarre or merely sly, the writer closest to Beckett's comedy is James Joyce, whose humour, like Beckett's, takes the form of allusions, digressions and wordplay, and who, like Beckett, was a Dubliner who emigrated and lived in Paris. Beckett has acknowledged his debt to Joyce: 'Joyce had a moral effect on me, he made me realise artistic integrity.'[12] They share an essentially poetic view of things, using allusive language and images to express the inexpressible, juxtaposed by exact descriptions of objects which are concrete and can be thus described. Most of all, they share a mischievous sense of fun, and are driven to manic laughter, particularly by their countrymen. Joyce said (*Letters*) that he wrote *Dubliners* to 'betray the soul of that hemiplegia of paralysis which many call a city'. *More Pricks than Kicks* owes something to *Dubliners*, and also sends it up. In 'The Dead', Joyce's hero dies after getting wet in the rain, while, characteristically, Beckett's hero in 'A Wet Night' merely gets a stomach-ache.

What Beckett especially admired in Joyce is his break, not only with traditional thinking, but with the conventions of language. In 'Dante . . . Bruno. Vico . . Joyce', Beckett says of Joyce's work: 'Here is direct expression', and agrees with Joyce that it is harmful 'to concentrate solely on the literal sense or even the psychological content of any document to the sore neglect of the enveloping facts themselves' (*Our Exagmination*, p. 13). Joyce has recognised the inadequacy of language and has replaced it by 'a quintessential extraction of language and painting and gesture' (p. 15). Bernard Shaw (*Letters*) disliked the realism of this method in *Ulysses* but admitted it was 'a truthful one'. Beckett particularly admired Joyce's objectivity: 'the fall of a leaf, the fall of a child, the fall of an empire, it was all one to him',[13] and it is an important part of Beckett's own method in 'telling it as it is'. Their closest relationship, though, is in the realm of irreverence, wild comedy and *non sequiturs*, which, for them, mirror life. Their humour was formed in Dublin, the home of such wit and word-play, blasphemy and obscenity, parody and paradox. Like Joyce, Beckett observes his fellow creatures, and finds comic material in their confusions. Most of all they share the joy of comic language. 'That's enough of finicking with Finnigan and fiddling with his faddles', says Joyce, and Beckett has a work called 'Foirade' in French and 'Fizzles' in English, which he said he 'farted out' and he gives the Oxford English Dictionary definition, 'The action of breaking wind quietly . . . a failure or fiasco'.[14]

Beckett shares with all these writers, and others, a compulsion to write to focus his ideas about the way things are. Like them he notes the ridiculous, and lampoons false illusions and complacency with a personal humour that throws new light on old themes. Philosophers from pre-Socratic times have also aided him in his task, providing him with quotations, or he has misquoted them, often from a humorous point of view. Beckett uses philosophers as he does the Bible, about which he says he uses its symbols because he is perfectly familiar with them,[15] though he doubts that philosophy and writing have anything to do with each other: 'The conception of Philosophy and Philology as a pair of nigger minstrels out of the Teatro dei Piccoli', he says, 'is soothing, like the contemplation of a carefully folded ham sandwich.'[16] Yet any assessment of twentieth-century writing must involve some consideration of philosophical influences in what Malraux calls 'ce domaine un peu troublé', where philosophy and fiction seem to come together.[17] Beckett uses the philosophical thoughts of others like a magic lantern, not to explain but to throw light upon life in his own time (maybe his own life) in the chaos and seemingly boundless, yet limited freedoms of the twentieth century.

The Ancient Greek philosophers have contributed an important part to Beckett's thinking. Most striking is the opposition of Heraclitus 'the sad philosopher', who saw existence as ever-changing, and Democritus, called 'the laughing philosopher' because he was amused by the follies of society and who is associated by Beckett with the clowns Bim, Bom and Grock (*More Pricks than Kicks*, p. 176). The pessimistic Belacqua, about to undergo minor surgery but fearing death, considers whether he should choose as mentor the humorist Democritus or the pessimistic Heraclitus, 'that pre-Socratic man of acknowledged distinction' whom he prefers. In order to make a good impression, 'do the little soldier', he decides on Democritus. 'He would arm his mind with laughter, laughter is not the word but it will have to serve' (p. 177). Ironically, because the anaesthetist has just returned drunk from a wedding, he does die. At the same time Heraclitus' image of life as flux is often used by Beckett, in whose works the eternal ebb and flow of the sea is a recurring symbol of an existence in which 'something is taking its course', and Heraclitus' 'dark sayings' are referred to in *Murphy* (p. 47). Zeno, 'the father of Stoicism', is 'that old Greek', in *Endgame* (p. 45). His analogy of life to a pile of millet seeds pattering down, is used by Hamm: 'Grain upon grain, one by one, and one day suddenly there's a heap, a little heap, the impossible heap.' This 'impossible heap', as the sum of life, is possibly what slowly engulfs Winnie in *Happy Days*. Throughout the works, Beckett makes mild fun of Pythagoras' theory that 'certainty' lies in numbers, often remarking what a comfort they are, and sending them up, for instance, in

Louit's thesis on the Visicelts, in *Watt*. A notable example of his comic use of mathematical formulas is the incident of the five biscuits consumed by a dog, as Murphy (*Murphy*, p. 73) considers the twenty different permutations in the order of eating them himself. Democritus' 'Nothing is more real than nothing' is one of Beckett's favourite quotations, and source of wit. Beckett himself has been compared to Diogenes, in exercising his 'mordant wit and vivid symbolism against the follies and vices of our age'. The orator continued: 'But this our modern Diogenes shows a greater compassion and humanity when he brings out the weaknesses into the light of truth, indeed his *Waiting for Godot* is in a sense a modern equivalent of the Psalmist's Expectans Expectavi.'[18]

As for religion, in the early works, Beckett inveighs, like Job, against the unfairness of Providence, to the point of blasphemy: 'So we drink Him and eat Him, watery Beaune and stale cubes of Hovis' (*Whoroscope*), or in *Murphy*: 'What but an imperfect sense of humour could have made such a mess of chaos' (p. 41). Yet, one of his favourite quotations is from St Augustine: 'Do not despair, one of the thieves was saved; do not presume, one of the thieves was damned', which Beckett describes as 'a fair percentage' (in *Murphy* and *Waiting for Godot*).

Beckett says that Christianity is a mythology with which he is perfectly familiar and so he uses it, and scriptural allusions are threaded throughout the works. In *Watt*, on his quest of Mr Knott, for example, although he has to retire baffled; like St Augustine, Watt comes to terms with his doubts (*Dubito ergo sum*), and becomes 'almost happy'. The Unnamable, too, infers he exists because he is unsure whether he exists, and decides not to decide: 'The best is not to decide anything in this connection, in advance. It's a thing that turns up for some reason or other, take it into consideration.' Although there is scepticism about God, there is recognition of the good in man, which Beckett expresses in Vladimir's care for Estragon, Camier's for Mercier.

On Descartes' *cogito ergo sum*, Beckett's thinking cripples are based. In *Waiting for Godot*, Estragon says: 'We always find something, eh Didi, to give us the impression we exist?' Cartesians to a man, divided in body and mind, like Murphy, 'through a deficiency of his conarium' (Descartes' pineal gland, which he thought regulated this division), Beckett's heroes escape from the 'colossal fiasco' of the world into dream. In his rocking chair,

Murphy's mind is 'body-tight'. This is 'true life' for Murphy, unfortunately denied him permanently because of the cravings of the flesh, which will not be denied. This division of body and mind is a source of anxiety and comedy throughout the works. When Watt's mental powers are not up to solving the enigma of the dogs who eat Mr Knott's leavings, he follows Descartes' advice (in *Rules for the Direction of the Mind*): 'When our understanding proves inadequate, we must stop, making no attempt to examine what follows.' Not being able to solve the mystery of Mr Knott himself, Watt retires into the dream world described by Descartes (in his *Sixth Meditation*); 'We cannot know with certainty at any one moment that we are not dreaming, but can only believe we are not, for our senses are not to be trusted.' Throughout Beckett's works there is the sense that it is all a dream, in which characters like Watt cannot decide 'between what happened and did not happen, between what was and was not.'

A disciple of Descartes', Geulincx, provided Beckett with a phrase, in 'beautiful Belgian Latin', which became one of his two recommended starting points for the study of his work: *ubi nihil vales, ibi nihil velis* (expect nothing where you are worth nothing). Beckett told Laurence Harvey in 1962 that if he were a critic setting out to write on the works of Beckett he would begin with quotations from Geulincx and Democritus, the 'laughing philosopher'. Beckett first read Geulincx's *Ethics* in 1930,[19] and a semi-autobiographical character ('The End', *Four Novellas*, p. 86) was given the *Ethics* by his tutor. Beckett freely exploits Geulincx's theory that true freedom can only be achieved by living in the mind, that energy should not be wasted in trying to control the external world, and that one should be indifferent to the passions. Murphy, for example, follows this precept while meditating in his rocking chair, but his love for Celia works against it, leading to his exchanging the meditative for the active life, and to his eventual downfall. Later characters, like Molloy, have less desire and, therefore, more freedom to live in their minds, and hold the world, if not events, at bay by this method. Molloy refers to this limited freedom (*Molloy*, p. 54). He has 'loved the image of old Geulincx, dead young, who left me free, on the black boat of Ulysses, to crawl towards the East, along the deck. That is a great measure of freedom, for him who has not the pioneering spirit.'

The power of thought is often the only power left to the later moribund characters, whose lives are but dreams, or nightmares which have their ludicrous moments.

On this aspect of existence as a dream, Beckett's thinking has much in common with that of Pascal, who sees life as a dream, only 'a little less inconstant' (*Pensées*, 386), and *Waiting for Godot* has been likened to 'Pascal's Pensées performed by the Fratellini Clowns'.[20] Because of its formlessness in time and space, its inconsequentialities, its repetitions, it has the qualities of a dream. Pascal attributes to the duality of man his doubts and uncertainties which bring about this sense of unreality, and sees the linking of mind and body as 'the consummation of man's difficulties'. 'How can man, who is only part of the whole, know the whole?', asks Pascal, and Beckett echoes this thought throughout the works. 'For what is man in nature?', asks Pascal (*Pensées*, 72) and answers: 'A nothing in comparison with the infinite, an all in comparison with the nothing, a mean between nothing and everything. Since he is infinitely removed from comprehending the extremes; the end of things and their beginning are hopelessly hidden from him in an impenetrable secret. He is equally incapable of seeing the nothing from which he was made, and the infinite in which he is swallowed up.' Like Beckett, Pascal sees uncertainty as man's natural condition: 'When we think to attach ourselves to any point, and to fasten to it, it eludes our grasp, slips past us and vanishes forever. Nothing stays for us' (*Pensées*, 72). Beckett illustrates this idea graphically in the losses and accidents suffered by his characters, who, nevertheless, survive by continuing to think. Pascal, too, concludes that 'thought constitutes the greatness of man' (*Pensées*, 346) because, however weak and deprived, man has the advantage over the rest of creation; he can think. 'All our dignity', says Pascal, 'consists then in thought' (*Pensées*, 347). Yet even thoughts are evanescent; on a lighter note Pascal and Beckett share an image, Pascal says (*Pensées*, 370): 'Chance gives rise to thoughts and chance removes them; no art can keep or acquire them. A thought has escaped me. I wanted to write it down. I write instead that it has escaped me.' Malone borrows this thought, when he records that three days of his squalid and uneventful life have gone unrecorded because he lost his pencil, and has just found it. Pascal provides a blueprint for Beckett's deprived thinkers: 'I can well conceive a man without hands, feet, head (for it is only experience that teaches us that the head is more necessary than feet). But I cannot conceive man without thought, he would be a stone or a brute' (*Pensées*, 339). The difference between *being* (the individual responsible for developing his own consciousness), and *existing* (like a vegetable or machine), is central to Beckett's theme. His cripples continue despite all the setbacks to think and to seek an identity.

Beckett flirts with other philosophies which flit fitfully throughout the works. We meet the shy shade of Bishop Berkeley, and his theories on materialism, in *Murphy*. His *'Esse est percipi'* comes in for some, often comic, treatment, and provides the leitmotif of *Film*. Beckett cheerfully sends up Schopenhauer, about whom he wrote in 1937: 'Like suddenly a window opened in a fog. Always knew he was one of the ones that mattered most to me.'[21] He shares Schopenhauer's scepticism, especially about Leibniz's idea that this is the best of possible worlds, and adapts Voltaire's phrase on the subject, 'So all things hobble together for the only possible' (*Murphy*, 127). He follows Schopenhauer in *Waiting for Godot*: Vladimir asks, 'What shall we do?' and Estragon says: 'Don't let's do anything, it's safer' (p. 18). But Beckett takes issue with Schopenhauer's out-and-out pessimism, when Schopenhauer says that, by silencing the will, we should be restored to peaceful non-existence. Not so, says Beckett, in a comic image, life would begin to 'ram her fish and chips down your gullet until you puke, and then the puke down your gullet until you puke the puke, and then the puked puke, until you begin to like it' (*Watt*, p. 48). 'Beginning to like it', Beckett seems to say, must be avoided at all costs.

Beckett has also adapted the ideas of Henri Bergson, on whom he lectured at Trinity College, Dublin in the 1930s. Bergson was the first main opponent of the concept of materialistic determinism inherited from the nineteenth century, against which Beckett in his oblique way is so active. More important, here, Bergson, possibly the only modern philosopher to write a book about comedy,[22] has provided notions which have furnished Beckett's humour. This is notably so in the plays, particularly *Waiting for Godot*, which uses the automatism, exaggerations, repetition, and circularity of plot which, for Bergson, are the essence of comedy. Social life, and human habits, have their humour, says Bergson (*Le Rire*, 24), and Beckett exploits this notion, for instance, in the mime, *Act without Words II*, in which two characters get up in the morning, dress, go out, return in the evening, undress and go back to bed, illustrating conventional life and habits, which do not seem grotesque until demonstrated theatrically. The exaggerations, and repetitions of *Waiting for Godot* provide a lighter side to the otherwise tragic situation of Vladimir and Estragon. The circularity of the plot, which gives the audience a sense of going somewhere, only to arrive at the point of departure, has a comic effect, which makes it clear that this is tragi-comedy. The conflicting needs of body and mind, says Bergson (*Le Rire*, 42), are comical: 'We laugh at the character who stops in the middle of a speech to complain of the tightness of his boots. The more paltry the claim of the body, the more striking the result.' In *Waiting for Godot* we have, for light relief, the boots and the urinating. Laughter, says Bergson, need not be just or kindhearted (*Le Rire*, 121), and Beckett's is often cruel. Bergson thinks that absurdity 'may have all the peculiarities of dream logic'; and that it may have the same effect as dreams on the subconscious, and arise from the same perturbations. In other words, such comedy has a carthartic effect, and it is significant that *Waiting for Godot* has been particularly appreciated by audiences 'outside society': prison inmates, and minorities in totalitarian states, or where freedom is threatened.

There are connections in Beckett's works with the humanistic aspects of existentialism which rose out of the anxieties of postwar France, and its emphasis on freedom of thought would appeal to the author of *Eleuthéria*. He has said: 'When Heidegger and Sartre speak of the contrast between being and existence they may be right, I don't know, but their language is too philosophical for me.'[23] Nevertheless, 'the difference between being and existence' is one of his main concerns, and he illustrates in his works the existentialist opposition to philosophies and ideologies which see man as without individuality, determined by external forces. The view that everyone must seek a means to survive life's eternal changes is expressed by Beckett throughout his works.

2

Beckett and the Theatre

In the long journey towards telling it as it is, and after completing the Trilogy, Beckett encountered the famous 'impasse' of language which brought him to a temporary halt in his writing. He asked: 'How can emotions, volatile and fluid by their very nature, be faithfully expressed in static, definite words? How can the inherently irrational and formless be given shape and order and still stay true to itself?'[1] The 'grisly afterbirth' of *The Unnamable*, *Texts for Nothing*, he said, did nothing to relieve the tension because it merely 'expressed the failure to implement the last words of *L'Innommable*, 'Il faut continuer, je vais continuer'.[2] He found a remedy for this tension in the theatre, because 'you have a definite space and people in this space, that's relaxing'.[3] Beckett's first play, *Eleuthéria*, never produced, had led to new self-discovery: 'I see a little clearly at last what my writing is about, and I fear I have perhaps ten years' courage and energy to get the job done. The feeling of getting oneself in perfection is a strange one after so many years of expression in blindness.'[4] About his second play, *Waiting for Godot*, Beckett said the words came easily, he simply wrote lines one after another: 'I was lucky that the dialogue sounded as good as it read.'[5]

As John Spurling has pointed out, the theatre was waiting for Beckett as Beckett was waiting for the theatre.[6] In the past century it has undergone a progression of changes which set the stage for Beckett's drama. The main innovators were Jarry, Artaud, and Pirandello, whose work did not depend on the contrivances of the 'well made play', but, on more allusive, poetic levels, on the perception and participation of the audience itself.

Although Jarry's plays are expressions of typical youthful iconoclasm, they were also seen as works of genius by, for instance, Mallarmé, and Apollinaire who believed such revolutionary, anti-realistic drama was instrumental in 'raising humanity above the mere appearances of things with which, left to itself, if it did not have geniuses who surpass it and point the way, it would have to be content'.[7] The plays were intended to shock the bourgeois audience out of its complacency, with obscenities, and knockabout rough humour. The actors were puppets on an open stage without curtains, not separated from the audience, Jarry wanted to make it, as in a circus, 'the macabre comedy of the English clown'. Yeats was shocked that the anti-hero king's sceptre was a lavatory brush, but prophesied that this debunking theatre would take the place of traditional forms of drama. 'After us', he said, 'the Savage God'.[8] It was Apollinaire who revived interest in Jarry's plays. He saw that, in the troubled climate of the 1920s, they would have relevance, because no-one was going to accept easy answers or solutions; that the portrayal of life on the stage must include this ambiguity, and that its tragic and comic aspects would have to be juxtaposed to produce not tragedy, but tragi-comedy. He wrote (in the preface to his *Breasts of Tiresias*) 'Depending on circumstances, tragedy will prevail over comedy or vice versa. But I do not think from now on that you will be able to endure, without impatience, a theatre piece in which these elements are not balanced against each other, for there is such an energy in mankind today . . . that the greatest misfortune immediately seems understandable, as though it may be considered, not only from the viewpoint of a kindly irony which permits laughter, but also from the perspective of a true optimism which at once consoles us and makes way for hope.'

Antonin Artaud, poet, actor and editor of *La Révolution Surréaliste*, was also impressed by Jarry's innovation, and wrote in *Nouvelle Revue Française* (November 1926): 'It is not to the mind or the senses of our audience that we address ourselves but to their whole existence. Theirs and ours.' He continued, 'For the theatre is the double of life, life is the double of true theatre . . . The double of the theatre is the reality which today's mankind leaves unusable.' In an interview with Israel Shenker,[9] Beckett took up this notion: 'My little exploration is that whole zone of being that has always been set aside by artists as something unusable – as something by definition incompatible with art.'

What Artaud wanted from the audience was an emotional, as well as an intellectual response. He saw the director's role as poet, interpreting the play, not the words only, but the non-verbal aspects; movements and gestures, use of space, and involving the audience in his perceptions. This arousal of intuitive perception is one of the most important factors in modern drama, and is particularly relevant in Beckett's plays, where the audience is by turns frightened, amused, bored, or disgusted, at what, in 'real life', they might rationalise. This 'gut reaction' is what Artaud referred to when he wrote: 'The theatre is the state, the place, the point where we get hold of man's anatomy.'[10] Beckett shares this notion, he described *Endgame* (in *Village Voice*, 19 March 1958) as 'rather difficult and elliptic, mostly depending on the power of the text *to claw*'. What they portray is man's defiance of what Artaud called 'the implacable cruelty of the universe',[11] which is universally experienced and which, once accepted, can be disarmed. Important elements in this portrayal are anarchy, incongruities which turn sense upside down, and ambiguities.

A strong link between Artaud and Beckett is their shared conviction of the inadequacy of words as a means of expression. In a letter to the editor of the *Nouvelle Revue Française* (28 September 1932) Artaud wrote: 'Words do not wish to say everything. By their nature and because they are fixed once and for all, they stop and paralyse thought instead of allowing it free play and encouraging it to develop.'[12] In his struggle with language Beckett expressed a similar thought about words: 'each time one wishes to make them express something other than words, they align themselves in such a way as to cancel each other out'.[13] As a remedy, Artaud calls for a true language of theatre, of shapes, movement, gesture, lights, in which words are not all-important. 'It is not a matter of suppressing speech in the theatre but of changing its role, and especially of reducing its position.'[14] The important thing was the 'gut reaction', akin to poetry; tragic, lyric, epic and comic. This is what Beckett's plays convey. So, indeed, do the novels. They have much in common with the drama in the images they evoke which are so much stronger than words.

From his earliest days of writing, Beckett has proclaimed the 'autonomy of the poetic vision' which he has displayed in his plays.[15] His own poetic vision shows the influence of the symbolists, and the surrealist movement, with which he was involved in Paris in the early 1930s. In a review of the work of the Irish poets, Denis Devlin and Brian Coffey, he praises them for 'submitting themselves to the influence of Corbière, Rimbaud, the Surrealists and Mr Eliot perhaps also to Mr Pound'.[16] Life was not to be muffled in comfortable clichés, and ambiguities were an important part of expression, as Beckett put it, the time had come 'for the vile suggestion that art has nothing to do with clarity, does not dabble in the clear and does not make clear'.[17] From the beginning, it was never Beckett's intention to tie his meanings down to mere words: 'The experience of my reader', he wrote, 'shall be between the phrases, in the silence, communicated by the intervals, not the terms.'[18] This allusive, poetic method in drama, Beckett shares with Pirandello, to whose works Walter Starkie, his tutor in Italian at Trinity College, Dublin, introduced him in 1926–7. Beckett also shares Pirandello's acute 'sense of opposites', tragedy and comedy, the many faces of truth, and the multiplicity of identities in any character. The relationship between Beckett and Pirandello was perceived by Jean Anouilh in a review of *Waiting for Godot* (in *Arts*, December 1953). Walter Starkie wrote, in 1926, 'To Pirandello belongs the credit for having explored the maze of the new technological age.'[19] Pirandello had made a new art, placing the human psyche in a man-made environment which added a dimension to the drama of the twentieth century, and prepared the way for Beckett and Ionesco, and later writers who work in the same genre.

Beckett inherits Pirandello's dramatic method and also some of his themes, his anti-heroes, his approach to sex and religion. Starkie says that Pirandello sees man as 'a fallen angel cast into the darkest abode of evil, rolling about in the mud and filth'.[20] He continues: 'Pirandello's anti-heroes suffer from a perpetual sense of disquiet which arises from the continual riddle which their personality propounds'.[21] Beckett's anti-heroes suffer in the mud the same disquiet, in their quest for identity in a shifting world. Pirandello saw existence as 'a labyrinth where our soul wanders through countless conflicting paths, without ever finding a way out. In this labyrinth I see a two-headed Hermes which with one face laughs and with the other weeps; it laughs with one face at the other's weeping.' And Beckett's heroes balance between laughter and tears, as they wander aimlessly, trying without success to hold back the current which sweeps them on. Pirandello shares his humorous view and envy of madmen, who opt out of this process: 'Ah, lucky madmen, who construct without logic, or else with a very special logic of their own' (*Henry IV*). Beckett's Murphy envies Mr Endon in the Magdalen Mercy Seat his 'very special logic of his own'.

The chief link between Pirandello and Beckett is humour, and their use of comedy in manipulating the reactions of the audience. Pirandello says how this is done: 'Imagine an old lady – we are

disposed to by sympathetic. But she is overdressed and painted –
we are ready to laugh. Yet she knows she is comical and does it to
attract her wayward husband – we are sobered. The old lady
seems pathetic again and the laugh is on us. The comic may be
no laughing matter.'[22] For Beckett, too, the comic is often no
laughing matter. As Nell says in *Endgame*: 'nothing is so comical
as unhappiness'. For Lucky, in *Waiting for Godot*, life is 'an abode
of stones . . . in spite of the tennis'. Comedy and tragedy are
intertwined.

About this mixture of farce and tragedy in Pirandello, Starkie
says: 'It is as if the author wanted us to look beyond his stage of
the comedy towards the true moral of his play which is a tragic
one. Such plays impose a severe tax on the mentality of the
ordinary theatre-going public. If they look at the play as a tragedy,
they find it difficult to reconcile their view with the air of comic
persiflage that pervades the majority of the scenes.' The same
difficulty is experienced by Beckett's audiences, but this mixture
of laughter and tragedy, and their evanescence, is a conscientious
attempt to tell us that that is what existence is about. Pirandello
puts this into a Beckettian phrase: 'We're here today, gone
tomorrow. A breath and we pass on to make room for others. That
cripple there . . . hobbling to his death on crutches. . . . Life
crushes someone's foot, rips out someone's eye. Peg-leg, glass-
eye, move along please!' Beckett echoes this laconic style in
Mercier and Camier, speaking of the long process of dying, and
what comes after, 'And to follow? That will be all, thank you. The
bill' (p. 109).

Beckett and Pirandello have a shared compulsion to tell it as it
is. Starkie says of Pirandello: 'He separates the real from the ideal
in a manner contrary to his predecessors, who held that the
function of the artist was to combine them in an artistic synthesis',
and Beckett has defined the duty of the artist 'to seek a new form
which will admit the chaos, and does not try to say that chaos is
really something else.'[23] Both playwrights are trying, in this way,
to show a true picture of existence, in all its shades from dark to
light, as experienced by the particular artist. This subjective view
was advocated by Pirandello who thought it takes a poet to draw
from language an individual form: 'the hollow word being
invested and animated by a particular feeling of the writer'.[24]

The great Irish writers share this subjective view of existence,
and poetic vision in expressing it. As Yeats put it, 'the necessity of

putting a life that has not been dramatised into their plays' stirs the Irish imagination: 'All art is founded upon personal vision and the greater the art the more surprising the vision.'[25] Beckett's admiration for Yeats, Synge and O'Casey is well-known. He shares their sense of the contradictory nature of existence, and is sensitive to the generation of the writers of the 1920s and 1930s who lived through the Troubles and proclaimed in their art what was wrong with Ireland. He shares their sense of black comedy. Reviewing Sean O'Casey's *Windfalls*, Beckett described him as 'a master of the knockabout in this very serious and honourable sense – that he discerns the principle of disintegration in even the most complacent solidities'.[26]

O'Casey's deprived people have much in common with Beckett's, particularly his prostitute, Jannice (*Within the Gates*), who is sister to Murphy's Celia, or to Lulu in *First Love*. Jannice is 'too generous and sensitive to be a clever whore, and her heart is not in the business', and Celia, who also dislikes her profession, is reproached by her grandfather for 'neglecting her work' for Murphy. O'Casey was an innovator in the presentation of serious themes as tragi-comedy. G. B. Shaw recognised this and praised it: 'There is a new drama rising from unplumbed depths to sweep the nice little bourgeois efforts of myself and my contemporaries into the dustbin.'[27] Like Beckett, O'Casey is keenly aware of the duality of life, which he describes as 'a lament in one ear maybe, but always a song in the other'.[28] Games with words, a sense of the grotesque and macabre, a black humorous attitude, are all aspects of great Irish writing, and so is irreverence: 'No aspect of life is too sacred', says Vivian Mercier, 'to escape the mockery of Irish laughter.'[29]

In *More Pricks than Kicks* (p. 100) Belacqua, about to weep, notices a grove of larch trees and, taking a rise out of Synge's love of nature, becomes more cheerful. Beckett shares with Synge the Irish gift for words, a love of mischief, fantasy, and ribaldry. Synge says, in the Preface to his *Playboy of the Western World*: 'Anyone who has lived in real intimacy with the Irish peasantry will know that the wildest sayings in this play are tame indeed, compared with the fancies one may hear in any little hillside cabin in Geesala, or Carraroe or Dingle Bay.' Beckett's works, especially the early ones, bear this out.

A modern dramatic medium which has influenced Beckett's theatre is the cinema, which in the 1920s and 1930s was a thrilling new experience, for Beckett as for others. It has been described as 'pure abstraction . . . not static but with all the resources of movement, change, rhythm, space, completely fluid to the will of the artist'.[30] This fluidity of technique is ideal for a writer whose theme is endless change. Ernest Betts has noted this: 'Heraclitus it was, who first perceived that all life consisted of, and tended towards change, and change is the first principle of all cinematography. The film is unique among the visual arts in postulating perpetual fluidity, or becoming, as the basis of conception.'[31]

Beckett has been interested in film techniques from their early days. Murphy's moment of birth is made into a cinematic image: 'he was projected . . . on the sky of that regrettable hour as on a screen, magnified and clarified into his own meaning' (*Murphy*, p. 104). The pot-poet, Ticklepenny, is seen by Murphy 'as though thrown on the silver screen by Griffith in midshot, soft focus' (p. 108). Beckett used silent film techniques in *Film*, with Buster Keaton, and has incorporated film lighting techniques in several plays. Film humour is adopted as part of his craft: Vladimir and Estragon wear Chaplin's clothes, Krapp slips on a banana skin, in *Watt* there is a pun on the 'hardy laurel', and cinema comics have embellished much of the non-verbal comedy of the works.

3

The 'Impasse' of Language

As the development of the comedy throughout the works may be seen as an indication of Beckett's philosophical trajectory, so his use of language mirrors the stages of his battle with words, the inadequacies of which are a main cause of his discomfiture, and, in the early and middle works, therefore, a rich source of comedy, composed of youthful wit, intolerance, verbosity, poetry and intellectual humour. In the middle works, the adoption of French as his medium had a disciplining effect, though the comedy persisted, generally in the juxtaposition of intellectual and colloquial language, irony and black humour. This stage eventually ran into the 'impasse' of what he called the 'total disintegration' of *The Unnamable*, and paradoxically, also to the relief of the drama, which revived the comic muse with its scope for non-verbal humour and knockabout in *Waiting for Godot*, led to the later more serious 'laugh at what is unhappy' of *Krapp's Last Tape* and *Endgame*, and culminated in the gnomic 'summing up' of *How It Is*, in which he felt he had said all he had to say, and his pensum was completed.

Reflection upon language and its problems is one of the oldest preoccupations of man. One of the earliest thinkers on the subject, Gorgias of Lentini (484–375 BC) said: 'there is nothing which has real existence; if there were, it could not be known; and supposing it were knowable, it could not be put into words'. For Beckett, the first proposition was decided by Democritus: 'Nothing is more real than nothing', which he told Colin Duckworth was his favourite quotation.[1] It is Gorgias' second premise, 'that if there were anything which has real existence, it could not be known', which is the key to Beckett's preoccupation with the nature of reality, and he says, paraphrasing Proust, 'the only world that has reality and significance is the world of our own latent consciousness' (*Proust*, p. 13). As to the last premise, 'Supposing it were knowable, it could not be put into words', this is the proposition that Beckett wrestles with, as A. J. Leventhal says, 'in a cascade of affirmation and denial'.[2]

So Beckett's task is two-fold. Believing that nothing is more real than nothing, and that reality is in his own latent consciousness, he must draw on this unconscious, then, accepting the challenge of 'supposing it were knowable, it could not be put into words', he must put it into words. His method therefore is to mine his subconscious, putting his experiences in an exaggerated form into the experience of his creatures, and expressing it through their stream of consciousness. He draws on Joyce's method, of which he said: 'Here form is content, content is form. You complain that this stuff is not written in English. It is not written at all to be read, or rather it is not only to be read. It is to be looked at and listened to. When the sense is sleep, the words go to sleep, when the sense is dancing, the words dance' (*Our Exagmination*, p. 14).

Beckett's world is more fragmented and tortured than Joyce's. He asked, in the Addenda to *Watt*:

> who may tell the tale
> of the old man?
> weigh absence in a scale?
> mete want with a span?
> the sum assess
> of the world's woes?
> nothingness in words enclose?

and took on the task. So his world is the world of the old man, absence, want, woe and nothingness, because he wants to encompass experience, 'tell the tale'. This world, ignored by many writers, he sees is as much part of experience as are youth, love, pleasure and well-being. Yet he sees that life is not all dark. As he has remarked in *First Love*, it would be easier if it were. Tears and laughter, light and shade are all part of it, and so it is 'a mess'. To 'accommodate the mess', his writing is recondite, convoluted, grotesque, sometimes clear, sometimes obscure, sometimes tragic, sometimes comic, full of *non sequiturs*. Throughout, the dark tones are heightened, and lightened, with humour which distances what he finds painful, and keeps painful themes in perspective.

His language generally is allusive, poetic and thought-provoking. Real communication takes place, says I. A. Richards, 'when one mind so acts on its environment that another mind is influenced and in the other mind an experience occurs which is like the experience in the first mind and is caused by part of that experience'.[3] It is this kind of communication which Beckett seeks to make, and it involves wide areas of imagery and symbolism, calling for an intuitive as well as intellectual response. Unlike Joyce, of whom, Beckett says: 'every word, every sentence, every page, every chapter had meaning', Beckett's writings flow unchecked from his subconscious. He told Jack McGowran: 'I don't know where the writing comes from and I am often quite surprised when I see what I have committed to paper. Writing for me is an entirely different process than it was for Joyce.'[4] Yeats described this kind of presentation as 'a mysterious act, always reminding and half-reminding, doing its work by suggestion, not direct statement . . . a complexity of rhythm, colour, gesture, not space-pervading like the intellect, but a memory and a prophecy'.[5] The poetry of the symbolists, which has these qualities, was a genre important to Beckett, who translated several of Rimbaud's poems, including *Bateau Ivre*. Rimbaud saw the poet as visionary and martyr (an idea which Beckett uses in *How It Is*) and said:

> The poet turns himself into a seer through a long colossal, reasoned disarrangement of all the senses. Every form of love, of suffering, of madness; he probes himself, he consumes in himself all the poisons, retaining only their quintessences. Ineffable torture which calls for all his faith and superhuman strength. The great criminal, the great sufferer, the utterly damned, the supreme holder of knowledge! For he attains the unknown.[6]

Rimbaud thought such vision could not be expressed in normal language and invented a new one, not bound by grammar, syntax or logic, to express 'l'ineffable'. In 'L'Alchimie du Verbe' (*Une Saison en Enfer*) he said: 'I expressed silence, darkness; I noted the inexpressible.'[7] Beckett experiments with this kind of language – humorously in *Watt*, in the late works much more seriously – to express the inexpressible, or, as he says, 'eff the ineffable'. Rimbaud's struggle with language failed: 'Mon art', he said, 'est un impasse'. But Beckett, in a similar impasse, has persevered. 'You must say words, while there are any', he said in *The Unnamable*, because words are all we have to prove we exist, and our only means of leaving anything behind. He puts his frustration into a comic image: 'The attempt to communicate where no

communication is possible is . . . horribly comic', he says, 'like
the madness which holds a conversation with the furniture'
(*Proust*, p. 63). But he believes the attempt to do it must continue:
'I can't go on. I will go on', says The Unnamable.

Beckett's frustration with words is exacerbated by his respect
and care for them. He expresses this in 'Casket of Pralinen' (1931):

> Oh I am ashamed
> of all clumsy artistry
> I am ashamed of presuming
> to arrange words

and again in 'Cascando' (1936)

> The churn of stale words in the heart again
> love, love, love, thud of the old plunger
> pestling the unalterable
>   whey of words

Like Watt, he is obsessed by words, which at first he treats
humorously: 'Watt's need of semantic succour was at times so
great that he would set to trying names on things, and on himself,
almost as a woman hats' (*Watt*, p. 79). Later, in *First Love*, he
notes the trouble he has 'in trying to say what I think I know'
(p. 1). The Unnamable is almost inundated: 'I'm in words, made
of words, others' words.' An early draft of *How It Is*, twenty years
later, begins: 'It comes the word we're talking of words'.[8]

In the early works, Beckett starts his war on words with an
attack on traditional writing. *Murphy* begins: 'The sun shone
having no alternative, on the nothing new. Murphy sat out of it,
as though he were free, in a mew in West Brompton.' In *Watt*:
'The moon was up, it was not far up, but it was up. It was of an
unpleasant yellow colour. Long past the full, it was waning,
waning' (p. 28). 'Fine' writing is parodied: 'High above the
horizon the clouds were fraying out in long black strands, fine as
weepers' tresses. Nature at her most thoughtful' (*Mercier and
Camier*, p. 120). Or, mixing the mock-poetic and the grotesque:
Lambs were 'springing into the world at every minute, the grass
was spangled with scarlet afterbirths, the larks were singing, the
hedges were breaking, the sun was shining, the sky was Mary's
cloak, the daisies were there, everything was in order' (*More
Pricks than Kicks*, p. 109).

An important humorous aspect of Beckett's use of language is his mixture of 'literary' language and colloquialisms, clichés, slang and puns. This is particularly apparent in French, which he turned to, following *Watt*, because he felt he needed the discipline of a language other than English. A spin-off of switching to French was that he had a new language to play with. He found writing in French congenial; as early as *More Pricks than Kicks* he apologises for a gallicism, explaining: 'the creature thinks in French'. In *Murphy* he was already punning bilingually: 'Celia, il y a'. He enjoyed the musicality of French diminutives. His character, speaking of babies, which he disliked, refers to their 'landaus, cerceaux, sucettes, patinettes, trottinettes, pépés, mémés, nounous, ballons, tout leur sale petit bonheur, quoi'. The tone is low-comic, ending with the demotic 'quoi' (*'Expulsé'*, p. 23). In *L'Innommable*, Worm's noises are 'glouglous divers'. Beckett's French felicities are often lost when translated into English, even by himself; 'baume tranquille', for instance, becomes 'Ellimans Embrocation', in *The Unnamable*. On the other hand, the English pun, 'Murphy is most off his rocker when he is on his rocker', is lost in French.

Another important humorous aspect of Beckett's language lies in the use of long pseudo-intellectual speeches, sententiousness and flat cliché (for example in *Waiting for Godot*) to produce a monotonous effect. This is a parody of the monotony of everyday life, and a satire on mankind's passive acceptance of, and indolent attitudes to it. A scrupulous banality of style is often used to portray the banalities of mankind and of existence.

A facet of Beckett's use of language, which has offended many sensibilities, is the use of obscenities. These mirror what he sees as obscene in life and in human nature, just as he uses sententiousness and cliché to express its banality and monotony. In a letter to Barney Rosset of Grove Press (26 December 1957),[9] he protested when the censor wished to exclude some obscenities in *Endgame*: that The Lord Chamberlain was making his 'usual chamber-pot storm'. Beckett himself has described his works as 'a matter of fundamental sounds, made as fully as possible', and in Rabelaisian vein, he added, 'no pun intended'.

At his best, Beckett's light touch with language has both a poetic and humorous effect, one of the best examples being from *Watt* (pp. 45–6), which is about the passing of time and the repetitiveness of events. His use of language mirrors this:

The crocuses and the larch turning green every year a week before the others, and the pastures red with uneaten sheep's placentas and the long summer days and the new-mown hay and the wood-pigeon in the morning and the cuckoo in the afternoon and the corncrake in the evening and the wasps in the jam and the smell of the gorse and the look of the gorse and the apples falling and the children walking in the dead leaves and the larch turning brown a week before the others and the chestnuts falling and the howling winds and the sea breaking over the pier and the first fires and the hooves on the road and the consumptive postman whistling *The Roses Are Blooming in Picardy* and the standard oil-lamp and of course the snow and to be sure the sleet and bless your heart the slush and every fourth year the February débâcle and the endless April showers and the crocuses and then the whole bloody business starting all over again.

This passage, circular and long drawn out, reflects the 'tears and laughter' of existence.

After 1960, Beckett's use of language changes. His reductionist tendencies, expressed as early as 1931: 'The artistic tendency is not expansive, but a contraction' (*Proust*, p. 64), take over in the later works, which are usually expressed by a single voice, often from the tomb, in jumbled syntax, in which language as an instrument is cut to the minimum, and made incomplete, contradictory and ambiguous to express the incompleteness, contradictions and ambiguities of existence. In these works he achieved the long-sought 'final disintegration of the "I" ', and the use of 'language which is a mantic instrument which does not hesitate to adopt a revolutionary attitude towards words and syntax' of the Surrealist Manifesto which he had signed in 1932,[10] and the writer, as narrator, becomes a voice ceaselessly murmuring in the dark, briefly repeating what he has said before.

4
The Early Works (1930–45)

In tracing the development of Beckett's humour, it is useful to begin at the beginning. Although unpublished, these early works are important, not only as sources of the humour but also as sources of the matter, because, throughout the works, Beckett remains remarkably faithful to his early preoccupations. For instance, an unpublished essay composed around 1928, concerned an imaginary literary movement in Paris, 'Le Concentrisme' led by an imaginary poet, Jean du Chas,[1] who appeared later in *More Pricks than Kicks*. A perfect spoof, it was presented as a lecture to the Modern Language Society of Trinity College, Dublin, and was taken seriously. It begins: 'Monsieur vous êtes le premier a vous intéresser à cet imbecile. Voici tout ce que j'en sais', and du Chas is described as 'fils unique, illégitime et posthume d'un agent de change belge, mort en 1906 par suite d'une maladie de peau', a description which has undertones of *Malone Dies* and *Watt*. Born, like Beckett, on 13 April 1906, du Chas was 'un de ces esprits qui ne peuvent s'expliquer'. In 1929 there followed the 'Che Sciagura' satire,[2] whose title was passed on in *More Pricks than Kicks*, as 'What a misfortune', and which is based on a bawdy line from Voltaire's *Candide* (Chapter XI): 'Che sciagura d'essere senza coglione'. In the same comic tradition, in 1931, Beckett wrote a parody of Corneille's *Le Cid*, entitled *Le Kid*, which was performed at Trinity College, Dublin, in February 1931, with Beckett in the role of Don Diègue, using an umbrella as a sword. The manuscript is lost, but a review of the performance survives.[3]

About 1931 Beckett became interested in Samuel Johnson. Three notebooks survive, and the MS of a play, *Human Wishes* (the first Act only)[4] based on Johnson and Mrs Thrale, which includes the cat Hodge, and a drunken butler, Levett. The few pages of dialogue prefigure the dialogue in *Waiting for Godot*:

Mrs Williams	Words fail us.
Mrs Desmoulins	Now this is where a writer for the stage would have us speak, no doubt.

Mrs Williams	He would have us explain Levett.
Mrs Desmoulins	To the public.
Mrs Williams	The ignorant public.
Mrs Desmoulins	To the gallery.
Mrs Williams	To the pit.
Mrs Carmichael	To the boxes.

It was the beginning of his life-long interest in the dramatic possibilities of the theatre.

Beckett's first novel was begun in Paris in 1932, and later he mined it heavily for *More Pricks than Kicks*. It has an Irish background, and is a send-up of a romantic novel of the time. Its title plays on Tennyson's poem and Henry Williamson's novel, *A Dream of Fair Women*, which Beckett improved to *A Dream of Fair to Middling Women*.[5] Its main protagonist is Beckett's perennial idle hero, Belacqua. Belacqua appears again in 'Echo's Bones', a short story written in 1934. He continues his adventures, after death, having been, like the Belacqua of *More Pricks than Kicks*, 'bumped off by a Fellow of some Royal College of Surgeons'. This fledgeling Belacqua sits on his own tomb joking with the gravedigger, and is ravished, 'to his astonishment', by the seductive Zaborovna Privet, after dining on fried garlic and Cuban rum. He is forced to stand in for the impotent Lord Gall of Wormwood, in spite of his protest: 'would you have me made a father?'. Beckett described this work as 'bottled climates' and said he wrote it because he would have perished with boredom otherwise.

In 1935 Beckett wrote an article 'Censorship in the Saorstat', a satirical attack on the censorship laws in the Irish Free State. In it he mentions Joyce's *Ulysses* and 609 other books, including his own, on a censorship list dated 30 September 1935. It is obvious that he was seriously concerned, but he treated the theme humorously, a foretaste of the way in which he often deals in later works with the majority of life's frustrations.

On 26 July 1934, the *Times Literary Supplement* carried a sagacious review of Samuel Beckett's first published book, *More Pricks than Kicks* (1934):

The humour which Mr Beckett extracts from the trivial and vulgar incidents which make up Belacqua's career is largely achieved by bringing to bear on them an elaborate technique of analysis. An implicit effect of satire is obtained by embellishing the commonplace with a wealth of observation and sometimes erudition, alternated with sudden brusqueness. Belacqua is more of a theme than a character, an opportunity for the exercise of a picturesque prose style . . . Part of 'Draff' is transcribed from an earlier prose piece of Mr Beckett's which appeared in *transition* and showed strongly the influence of Mr Joyce's latest work – a dangerous model. There is still more than the setting of 'Dubliners' to remind us of this writer, but a comparison between the piece in *transition* and the present book shows how much Mr Beckett's work has gained from discipline of his verbal gusto. It is still a very uneven book; but there is a definite, fresh talent at work in it, though it is a talent not yet quite sure of itself. The chapter or episode which describes Belacqua in hospital, waiting for the doctors to give him 'a new lease of apathy', is perfect in its way, and there are few pages not enlivened by Mr Beckett's gift for apt extravagance. His humour, with its curious blend of colloquialism, coarseness and sophistication, is unlikely to appeal to a large audience.

Beckett himself looked on *More Pricks than Kicks* as juvenilia. He wrote to Barney Rosset of Grove Press in 1956 that he did not think the *More Pricks* stories worth bothering about, except perhaps 'Yellow',[6] and it was not reprinted until thirty years after its first appearance. The book is important, as the forerunner of all the works on the theme of the conflict between Beckett's heroes' desire to be individuals and escape society, and yet to be part of it. Belacqua, the prototype Beckett hero, makes his first published appearance in *More Pricks than Kicks*, which is based on the earlier, unfinished novel, *A Dream of Fair to Middling Women*. It is a rich collection of droll anecdotes, some autobiographical, about the 'sinfully indolent' Belacqua Shuah, beginning with his student days at Trinity College, Dublin, and ending with his death in early middle age. In a letter to the poet Thomas MacGreevy, Beckett said he wrote it because of a 'desperate itch to grub up my guts for publication'.[7] It was written soon after he left Trinity College as a prize scholar, and before he turned his back for good on home, Ireland, and academe. Beckett and Belacqua are closely related; the narrator tells us 'We were Pylades and Orestes for a period, flattened down to something very genteel' (*More Pricks*, p. 40), and much of the comedy comes out of his authorial interventions and sly comments on Belacqua's

character. He also tells us that in time he tired of Belacqua: 'He
was an impossible person in the end. I gave him up in the end
because he was not serious.'

Belacqua's trouble is that he will not grow up; and he remains
infantile to the end. However, his childishness is the source of
much of the comedy; he is not without charm. Beckett describes
him as 'a kind of cretinous Tom Jones' (p. 111). The young
Belacqua's pleasures are food and drink (at this age, stout). A
meal is described that would 'abide as a standard in his mind'.
When he ate it, 'his teeth and jaws had been in heaven' (p. 17).
There is a long comic description of how this memorable sandwich
is made. He is vindictive to the loaf: 'He laid his cheek against the
soft of the bread, it was spongy and warm, alive. But he would
very soon take that plush feel off it, by God, but he would very
quickly take that fat white look off its face' (p. 11). He makes two
equally burnt rounds, 'Not butter, God forbid' (p. 12). Buttered
toast, in Belacqua's view, is all right for 'Senior Fellows, with only
false teeth in their heads. It was no good at all to a fairly strong
young rose like Belacqua.' His whole being 'was straining towards
the joy in store', but there is a hiatus, he has forgotten the
gorgonzola. The narrator announces in scriptural tones: 'He had
burnt his offering but not fully dressed it'. On the way to the
grocer's, 'alone with his joyous anticipation', he dreads being
accosted. The narrator tells us that 'his hunger, more of mind, I
need hardly say, than body, amounted to a frenzy. Woe betide
the meddler who crossed him when his mind was really set on
this meal.' Obtaining the cheese, he hobbles off – Belacqua is the
first of a long line of heroes with 'a spavined gait' – 'his feet were
in ruins'. Growing older, Belacqua 'puts away a childish thing or
two' (in 'A Wet Night'), and his tipple changes from stout to
brandy, but it is still as an infantile image, 'a breast', that he
thinks of the bottle in his pocket (*More Pricks*, p. 75). To make
sure the allusion is not missed, it is mentioned three pages later
as 'a breast of Bisquit' (p. 78).

In 'A Wet Night', the bourgeoisie and pseudo-intellectuals of
Dublin inspire vindictive comedy, rich in characterisation. There
is a Professor of Bullscrit and Comparative Ovoidology, who
'bombles'. He shares with women who talk too much, like Winnie
(in 'Fingal'), the reproof: 'Who shall silence them at last?'. Beckett
is more sardonic about the academic, and asks, 'who shall
circumcise their lips from speaking at last?'. The oversexed and

avant garde Caleken Fricka, who 'frankly itches to work that which is not seemly', grasps 'in her talons the works of Sade'. The worldly Countess Parabindi is 'very much the lone bird' at the party, 'in the absence of her husband, the Count, who had been unable to escort her on account of his being buggered if he would' (p. 71). Beckett has it in especially for whimsy Irish writers of 'prosodoturfy', or the singer Larry Murcahaoda, 'who tore a greater quantity than seemed fair of his native speech-material to flat tatters' (p. 84). There is also the rural figure of a poet 'in Wally Whitmaneen Donegal tweeds, who gave the impression of having lost a harrow and found a figure of speech', and three lesser poets 'with Lauras to match' (p. 70). The poets are not Petrarchs, and the Lauras not Laura; or another poet, from the middle-west, whose drawl is 'like an ogleful of tears'. In 'What a Misfortune' we meet the forerunners of Beckett's grotesques, James Skyrm, 'an aged cretin', who 'gnashes his teeth without ceasing at invisible spaghetti' (p. 148), and the powerfully-built nymphomaniac cripple, Hermione Nautsche, the only relatives Belacqua can round up to support him at 'the nuptial jamboree'. They provide a comic sub-plot, by falling in love, like Watt and Mrs Gorman.

Nothing, not even religion, stirs Beckett to such pitiless mockery as a wedding. The layout of the invitation is compared to an epitaph 'with a terrible sigh in the end pause of each line. And yet . . . one might have expected a little enjambment in an invitation to such an occasion'; there is a pause for appreciation of sexual innuendo and intellectual snigger, reinforced by the authorial comment that the only thing wrong with the joke was 'its slight recondity, so few people knowing what an enjambment was'. There is more sexual innuendo: the wedding takes place in the Church of St Tamar, 'pointed almost to the point of indecency' (p. 147). At the altar there is a comic passage, full of images of doom and destruction (p. 148). Belacqua's heart 'makes a dash against the wall of its box'; the church becomes a 'cruciform cage'; 'the bulldogs of heaven' hold up the chancel, the transept is a cul-de-sac; the organist darts into his loft 'like an assassin'. Belacqua has a sense of 'being cauterised with an outward and visible sign' (not of inward, invisible grace). He passes the ring 'like a mouse belling the cat', and the service provokes him to 'a copious scoff that would have put the kibosh on the sacrament altogether had it not been for the coolness and skill of the priest who covered as with a hand this coarseness with a collect' (p. 150). At the reception, Mrs bboggs whips the muslin off the Delikatessen 'almost before the organist has regained control of his instrument'. Belacqua-in-love is an important source of comedy, which, in the early days ('Fingal'), takes the form of sexual innuendo. He is 'as wax' in Winnie's hands, she 'twists him this way and that'. When they have been on the hilltop for awhile he is 'a very sad animal indeed'. He fancies she looks Roman. 'Only pout', he begged, 'be Roman, and we'll go on across the estuary. And then . . .'. The narrator intervenes: 'And then! Winnie take thought'. We are told that Winnie is 'the last girl he went with before a memorable fit of laughing incapacitated him from gallantry for some time'.

There is a marked change in Belacqua's lovelife in 'A Wet Night', providing material for satire on female sexuality. Without desire himself, Belacqua is pursued by the nymphomaniac Caleken. When he returns, wet-through to her party, from his drunken walk in the rain, we are told that he derives 'the impression that something had inflamed her'. 'Every stitch', she gloated, 'must come off at once, this very instant'. To cool her ardour he asks for a towel, and the narrator tells us that 'Caleken, though deeply chagrined . . . knew her man well enough to realise that his determination to accept no more final comfort at her hands than the loan of the towel was unalterable.' Thus female sexuality is put down, but, on the other hand, the Alba is commended for keeping her admirers at the party from joining in 'the hugger mugger that spread like wildfire through the building'. He goes so far as to state: 'So that from the point of view of her Maker . . . she was quite a power for good.' But Belacqua's ineptitude is mocked. When the Alba says 'Take me home', he insists on a taxi, but has no money and she has to pay.

'Love and Lethe' is black, comic, rich in double-entendres. Belacqua has turned for comfort to Ruby, 'whose IT has run dry', and she tolerates his coldness, hoping that 'sooner or later, in a fit of ebriety or of common or garden incontinence, he would so far forget himself as to take her in his arms'. As an afterthought we are told that Ruby is incurably ill, she has been 'given up by fifteen doctors, ten of whom were atheists'. The author merely remarks, 'Even the most captious reader must acknowledge not merely the extreme wretchedness of Ruby's situation, but also the verisimilitude of what we hope to relate in the not too distant future' (p. 94). What he has to relate is that, far from wishing for a love affair, Belacqua, who, the author says, 'ought to be in a mental home' is hoping for a suicide pact – 'felo de se (the genteel term)' – because he could not do it 'on his own bottom'. He convinces her he is 'no greenhorn yielding to the spur of momentary pique but an adult desperado of fixed and even noble purpose', which puts her 'almost in a state of joy'. The author amplifies this: 'She was done in any case, and here was a chance to end with a fairly beautiful bang.' The irony is that the bang was not the bang she thought it would be (because the pistol misfires), and, though she does not lose her life, she gets what she wanted in the first place, because, to climb a fence on the way to the trysting place, she removes her skirt and 'storms the summit in her knickers', which distracts Belacqua. The narrator remarks sardonically 'how difficult things were becoming to be sure. The least thing might upset the apple-cart at this juncture.' He is right. After drinking a bottle of whisky they come together in 'inevitable nuptial' and, the narrator adds coyly, 'With the utmost reverence at our command, moving away on tiptoe, we mention this in a low voice.'

In 'Walking Out' the comedy becomes savage. The title is a pun on walking out, in the sense of courting, and Belacqua's walking out to escape it. Lucy has 'a morbid passion' for her intended husband, but Belacqua wishes her to take a lover. He himself wants only to watch other people's lovemaking in the wood. She suspects this and resolves to 'put him to the test', 'for of course he was as wax in her hands' (here the author puts a footnote referring to an earlier chapter: Cp. 'Fingal') (p. 116). This test however never takes place because, in a supreme understatement, Lucy is crippled for life by 'a superb silent limousine, a Daimler no doubt, driven by a drunken lord'. 'Tempus edax', they marry and live happily ever after and, as Lucy is crippled, the author remarks bathetically, 'the question of cicisbei does not arise'.

After this, Belacqua's love affairs go from bad to worse, for Thelma 'perished of sunset and honeymoon that time in Connemara' (p. 187), and Belacqua himself is soon to perish on the operating table. In his last hour the narrator is heavily ironical, for he knows Belacqua's moments are numbered: 'Poor Belacqua, he seems to be having a very dull irksome morning preparing for the fray in this manner. But he will make up for it later on, there is a good time coming for him later on, when the doctors have given him a new lease of apathy' (p. 174). When the unfortunate

Belacqua, euphoric from an injection, climbs 'like a bridegroom' onto the table it is the drunken anaesthetist, just returned from acting as best man at a wedding, who gives him away, for he dies under the anaesthetic.

Belacqua's trouble in love, as in everything else, is his lack of commitment, from which Beckett draws much, seemingly heartfelt, saturnine humour. He points out in explanation that Belacqua was a poet, and therefore not subject to conventional limitations. He illustrates poignantly the dilemma of such an unconventional-romantic character, particularly in love: 'A poet is indeed a very nubile creature, dowered, (don't you know) [a Wodehouse touch] with the love of love . . . . So nubile that the women, God bless them, can't resist them, God help them. Except of course those merely for breeding and innocent of soul, who prefer, as less likely to upset them, the more balanced and punctual raptures of a chartered accountant or a publisher's reader' (p. 128). This distaste for the role of the male in the conventional mating situation echoes again in Murphy's diatribe against Celia and the 'charVenus, sausage and mash sort of love'.

Belacqua is conscious of his solipsism, and consequent shortcomings in relation to other people. Leaving, in a dreamlike state, after his wedding he says doubtfully to himself: 'It is right that they who are loved should live' (p. 159), and we are told: 'It was from this moment that he used to date in after years his crucial loss of interest in himself as in a grape beyond his grasp.' Murphy, in his turn, when overpowered by his love for Celia, and so distracted from his desire to be alone, experiences the same feelings.

Murphy (1938) is not, like *More Pricks than Kicks*, a pyrotechnic display, but is a serious philosophical work. In a letter to Thomas MacGreevy of 17 July 1936 Beckett described his treatment of the book as 'a mixture of compassion, patience and mockery'.[8] Later when asked to shorten it for publication he said: 'If the book is slightly obscure it is because it is a compression . . . to compress it further can only result in making it more obscure. The wild and unreal dialogues, it seems to me, cannot be removed without darkening and dulling the whole thing. They are the comic exaggeration of what elsewhere is expressed in elegy, namely, if you like, the Hermeticism of the spirit . . . . There is no time and no space in such a book for the *mere* relief [Beckett's italics]. The relief has also to do work and reinforce that from which it relieves.

And of course the narrative is hard to follow. And of course deliberately so.' So, for Beckett, the relief of the comic exaggeration has a positive function. It has to do the work 'and reinforce that from which it relieves'.[9]

Given that the subject of the novel is not comic, and that the comedy has to 'reinforce that from which it relieves', the poignant effect of the comedy gives the book particular distinction in the canon because, in *Murphy*, we are on the way to the *risus purus*, being able to laugh at what is unhappy, and not to 'whinge'. In this way, *Murphy*, as Beckett has said, prefigures *Waiting for Godot*.[10] It is built on situations that could be tragic, except that they are lightened by cruelly comic or incongruous remarks, which mock despair.

While writing *Murphy*, Beckett was living in London, in the very streets now haunted by the ghosts of Murphy and Celia. This gives the location of the book a strong sense of immediacy and a brooding nostalgia. At the time, he was interested in Jungian psychology, and visited a 'mental mercy seat'. This asylum comes over strongly as a microcosm of the world itself, as Beckett sees it; a seat of unfair judgments and scant mercy. The main source of comedy in *Murphy* is its erudite, mocking tone, and intellectual *tours de force*, and much of the fun lies in the high-spirited word-play, puns, altered aphorisms, witty incongruities and outrageous irony. There is some very acute characterisation, and appreciation of human absurdities.

Although Murphy, especially in his rocking chair, shares the Belacqua fantasy that 'just beyond the frontiers of suffering lies the landscape of freedom', he is not a merely indolent man like Belacqua. He has a 'metaphysical' reason for trying to avoid work; it would destroy him as an individual. And we are told that 'the only thing Murphy was seeking was what he had not ceased to seek from the moment of his being strangled into a state of respiration – the best of himself' (p. 44). He sums up his dilemma for Celia. He has her, his body and his mind, and he tells her: 'In the mercantile Gehenna . . . one of these will go, or two, or all. If you, then you only; if my body then you also'; (after all without a body he would not have much use for Celia); 'if my mind, then all' (pp. 26–7). Murphy has the same objection to marriage; that it would destroy him as an individual, and he blames women, who 'abolish love' for 'brats and house bloody wifery'. The author intervenes here: 'An atheist chipping the deity is not more senseless than Murphy defending his course of inaction.' Murphy, too, does a fair amount of senseless chipping at the deity.

Murphy's chief problem is that he is divided. The body (which he detests) longs for Celia, the mind (which he loves) 'shrivels at the thought of her', an apposite innuendo. However, he decides to marry her, and comes across a second, equally important problem, money. 'Celia spent every penny she earned and Murphy earned no pennies' (p. 15). So far he has managed on a pittance from a Dutch uncle (Mr Quigley, his uncle, lives in Holland), but it is not enough for two, and he dare not appeal for more. 'Shall I bite the hand that starves me', said Murphy, 'to have it throttle me?' Mr Quigley most certainly would not increase his allowance, and might stop it entirely. Murphy prefers to keep the status quo, rather than lose all. When Celia points out that they cannot continue without money, Murphy says that Providence will provide. 'The imperturbable negligence of Providence to provide' makes them fall about laughing, which prefigures the old couple confronted with a similar text in *All that Fall*.

An important aspect of Beckett's early comic method is the digression which holds up the action, lightens a dark passage, or provides a release in tension and a reassurance that nothing is as bad as it might seem. In his dire predicament – having to work to keep Celia – there is the humorous digression of the horoscope. Murphy decides to put it to his stars, and sends Celia to buy a sixpenny horoscope in Berwick Market from a seer, Ramaswami Krishnaswami Narayanaswami Suk, who advertises himself as 'Famous throughout the Civilised World and Irish Free State'. This horoscope contains such gems, on the subject of Murphy's character, as: 'Intense Love nature prominent, rarely suspicioning the Nasty, with inclinations to Purity'. It suggests a career as a 'promoter, detective, custodian or pioneer'. 'Lucky Colours. Lemon. Lucky Days. Sunday. Lucky Years 1936 and 1990.' Cheered by this, Murphy decides that 'the first 4th to fall on a Sunday in 1936' he will wear a yellow bow tie and go 'to custode, detect, explore, pioneer, promote or pimp as occasion may rise', and accuses Celia of pushing him into the 'mercantile gehenna'. When she asks why the horoscope comes in a black envelope, Murphy replies that it is 'because this is blackmail' (p. 22).

At the end of a day looking for work, Murphy hastens back to Celia (p. 62), 'it had been a trying day for Murphy in the body and he was more than usually impatient for the music to begin'.

He arrives to find not 'a meal spoiling as he had hoped and feared', but Celia spreadeagled face down on the bed: 'A shocking thing had happened'. On this note of suspense we are confronted with a digression, a whole chapter, on Murphy's mind, headed *'Amor intellectualis quo Murphy se ipsum amat'* (the intellectual love with which Murphy loves himself), a misquotation from Spinoza. This digression creates a comic hiatus and the chapter ends with the authorial comment: 'This painful duty having now been discharged, no further bulletins will be issued' (p. 66).

The digression of the chess game relieves tension in Murphy's sad first night on duty, when he feels locked out of the sleeping 'microcosmopolitan world' of the Magdalen Mental Mercy Seat. To be excluded from the 'little world' is a particularly harsh blow for Murphy, whose 'old refrain' was 'I am not of the big world, I am of the little world' (p. 101). Trudging with a heavy heart through the corridors he discovers 'the most biddable little gaga in the entire institution', his favourite, Mr Endon, playing chess. This enlivens Murphy's rounds (patients have to be spied upon every twenty minutes throughout the night) because he is able to return, after each tour, to make a move in the game. He hastens the rounds to finish ahead of time: a round finished on time was called a virgin; ahead of time an Irish virgin, and 'never in the history of the MMM had there been such a run of virgins and Irish virgins as on this Murphy's maiden night'. The game, called 'Endon's Affence', or 'Zweispringerspott', is set out in detail, move by move, with comments like: '(a) Mr Endon always played Black. If presented with White he would fade, without the least trace of annoyance away into a light stupor', or, '(e) Ill-judged', or, '(h) Exquisitely played'. At the end, which is of course inconclusive, Mr Endon merely up-ends his King and Queen's Rook, and '(r) Murphy, with Fool's Mate in his soul, sinks too into a trance . . . at peace, an unexpected pleasure' in that 'Nothing, than which in the guffaw of the Abderite nought is more real' (p. 138). This 'guffaw' (nothing is more real than nothing), Beckett has called 'one of the two important points in *Murphy*'.[11]

The digressions in *Murphy* were important to Beckett. Writing to the publisher, George Reavey, about suggested cuts in the book, he refused to remove the sections on Murphy's mind, or the game of chess. The horoscope chapter, he said, was essential, though he offered to change the title (which was considered too

Irish) to 'Quigley, Tromhebereschlein, Eliot, or any other name the publishers fancy'. The reason he could not give up these digressive passages, he said, was that the book would 'lose what resonance it had without them'.[12]

A resonant note is struck by Murphy's and Celia's affair. Soon after they meet 'on the corner of Cremorne Road and Stadium Street' (where Murphy was star-gazing and Celia was 'going about her business', soliciting), they become inseparable. 'Celia loved Murphy, Murphy loved Celia; it was a striking case of love requited' (p. 13), and he proposed the following Sunday in Battersea Park sub-tropical garden. From June to October their nights were 'harmonious' – a play on 'music' – 'serenade, nocturne and albada' until Celia (although she shrinks from 'a profession she had always found dull') (p. 41), says that, if he does not find work, she will have to go back to hers. 'Murphy knew what that meant. No more music. The phrase is chosen with care', the author tells us, 'lest the filthy censors should lack an occasion to commit their filthy synecdoche'. The star-crossed lovers part.

At such times of trouble, Murphy 'recruited himself in the Archaic Room, British Museum', appropriately, as his trouble is a woman, 'before the Harpy Tomb' (p. 51). Celia loves Murphy, and worries that he sees her as 'a Fury' (or harpy) 'coming to carry him off, or even a tipstaff with warrant to distrain. Yet it was not she, but Love, that was the bailiff. She was but the bumbailiff' (p. 19) or love's lackey. It is all the fault of love, the author points out. Murphy needs Celia. He does not have heart attacks, or need to tie himself to his chair when she is with him. He tells her so, 'keeping back nothing that might alarm her' (p. 21). Even when their affair is almost at an end, he cares enough for her to enjoy 'cutting the tripes out of her'. When he goes off to work at the MMM, Celia feels he is going out of her life. She is right, as it turns out, because he finds happiness in the 'little world' of the institution.

But later, on night-duty, he loses the company of the 'microcosmopolitans', and feels excluded because of the gulf between him and them. He needs his chair once more, and fetches it from Brewery Road when Celia is out. Rocking in his chair, Murphy has a vision. The letters MMM rise before his eyes but, instead of representing Magdalen Mental Mercy Seat, which has been his haven up to now, he sees that they stand for Music, MUSIC, MUSIC. The author puts a note here for the 'gentle compositor', asking him to print this in 'brilliant, brevier and canon, or some such typographical scream' (p. 132), and tells us that 'Murphy interpreted this in his favour, for he had seldom been in such need of encouragement'. Murphy at last sees that love and Celia are the answer, and this is where the second key text in *Murphy* comes in, which Beckett offers us from Geulincx: *Ubi nihil vales, ubi nihil velis* (where you are worth nothing want nothing). Murphy turns this on its head. He sees that where he is worth something (to Celia), is where he should want something, though ironically he is to die before he can return to her. This is a very stylish vignette of an unsuccessful love affair, which prefigures the one, equally unachieved, in the satirically named *First Love*.

The dialogue looks forward to the dramatic works and its stychomythic rhythms add considerably to the comic potential of the novel. The combination, in *Murphy*, of cruel observations and comic exaggeration, in elegantly ironic prose, mixing literary language and colloquialisms, certainly has the effect, which Beckett hoped for, of not only 'relieving, but reinforcing that from which it relieves'. *Murphy* is not a merely comic or frivolous novel, but is, as Beckett said: 'a mixture of compassion and mockery'. Beckett is beginning to perfect not only his comic method, but also the expression of the idea that 'perhaps' and 'a sense of proportion' are key words in an existence made up of antinomies and uncertainties, and that not to 'whinge' is an important step in the philosophical progression towards the *risus purus*, the laugh that laughs at what is unhappy. As Beckett has remarked, Murphy 'never whinges'.

The tone of Beckett's next novel, *Watt*, written in exile in southern France during the Occupation (it was published in 1953) is much darker. The youthful gloom and bawdy high spirits gave way to more serious undertones and cruel humour. In *Watt* it is the turn of the earnest seeker for the meaning of existence to be parodied and ridiculed. Seeking certainties, solely for his own peace of mind, Watt attempts to rationalise all the mysteries he meets with. Unlike Belacqua and Murphy with whom, up to a point, the author identifies, Watt is not an individual. His point of view, not that of a free thinker, depends upon conventional ideas. The book demonstrates the weakness of this point of view in the face of the paradoxes of existence, and the author is less tolerant in his dealings with this hero: 'one wonders sometimes', he says sardonically, 'where Watt thought he was. In a culture park?' (p. 73).

Watt fails to come to terms with his circumstances, and with the lack of explanations in his world. Towards the end of his stay in Mr Knott's establishment he learned to accept it, to bear it, 'and even in a shy way to like it', we are told, 'But then it was too late'. It is a *sine qua non* for the Beckett hero that he should not only survive, but have an imaginative and positive approach, however wretched his existence, and Watt fails in this. Even his account of Mr Knott's house is far from clear, the narrative structure is odd, out of sequence, 'Two, one, four, three – that was the order Watt told his story'. The narrator adds ironically: 'Heroic quatrains are not otherwise elaborated' (p. 214). There are no heroic quatrains, Watt is not that kind of person, and it is not that kind of book. The useful Addenda are marked: 'The following precious and illuminating material should be carefully studied. Only fatigue and disgust prevented its incorporation' (p. 247). As previously, authorial interventions are illuminating and heighten the comic effect.

However, the most important thing about *Watt* is that this is the work in which we are first made aware of the theme which Beckett develops so devastatingly in his later works, the impossibility of true communication: that 'What we know partakes in no small measure of the nature of what has so happily been called the unutterable or ineffable, so that any attempt to utter or eff it is doomed to fail' (p. 61). Nevertheless, as Beckett and his heroes (even Watt) demonstrate in their tireless efforts to say it like it is, one has to go on trying.

In *Watt*, the eponymous hero seeks to discover what experiences 'might be induced to mean, with the help of a little patience, a little ingenuity' (p. 72) in a world he does not understand. Beckett described *Watt*, written in hiding in occupied France, as 'only a game, a means of staying sane, a way to keep my hand in . . .'. However, he also said that it 'has a place in the series'. In a letter to George Reavey, Beckett wrote: 'It is an unsatisfactory book, written in dribs and drabs, first on the run, then of an evening after the clod-hopping, during the occupation, but it has a place in the series, as will perhaps appear in time.'[13]

Watt certainly has an important place in the canon. It develops the serious themes in *Murphy* and, just as Murphy is heir to Belacqua, so Watt is Murphy's heir. We are told that when Watt could not sleep he sometimes rose in the small hours to look at the stars 'which he had once known familiarly by name, when dying in London' (p. 212). However, *Watt* is quite unlike *Murphy*. Its texture is more dense and its preoccupations darker. Watt's sojourn in Mr Knott's establishment is possibly an image of the purgatory of worldly existence, and Watt's garbled account of it perhaps illustrates the confusion of human understanding. There are images of alienation in the uncertainties of time and place, in the surrealistic absence of transition passages between episodes, and in the *non sequiturs* of Watt, as he disintegrates under the strain of trying to understand and express the ineffable. It is not surprising that Sam finds Watt tedious. He is a dull and fatuous character, the prime example of Beckett's category of 'non-doers' and, without Sam, even his observations of Mr Knott's world would have been lost to posterity. The main themes of *Watt* are the cruelty of the universe, the nature of the deity, and the difficulties of communication. The tone alternates between devil-may-care wit, horror comedy, and Lewis Carroll fantasies.

Watt's discoveries in Mr Knott's establishment are told at second-hand by Sam, who doesn't rate Watt very highly as a reporter. Sam makes a disclaimer about the information he receives from Watt, whom he describes as an 'imperfect witness', and excuses himself for the sparseness of the information, saying that Watt had difficulties in recalling what happened in Mr Knott's house: 'it was a long time past . . . . Add to this the obscurity of Watt's communications, the rapidity of his utterance and the eccentricities of his syntax' (p. 72). Watt's weakness is that 'he desired words to be applied to his situation', 'to Mr Knott, to the house, the grounds, his duties . . . and in a general way to the conditions of being in which he found himself' (pp. 77–8). This is given a comic image: 'Watt's need of semantic succour was at times so great that he would set to trying names on things, and on himself, almost as a woman hats' (p. 79). Watt, then, is probably the forerunner of the story-tellers in the later works, but he cannot get it together himself, so is forced to tell it all to Sam.

It is the lack of explanation of phenomena which troubles the pedestrian Watt: 'The most meagre, the least plausible, would have satisfied Watt, who had not seen a symbol, nor executed an interpretation since the age of fourteen, or fifteen, and who had lived, miserably it is true, among face values all his adult life'

(p. 70). Watt cannot accept incidents 'for what they perhaps were, the simple games that time plays with space . . . he was obliged, because of his peculiar character to enquire into what they meant' (pp. 71–2). For Watt, to explain is to exorcise. If he can classify things they cease to worry him, so he tries to preserve his peace of mind with a succession of hypotheses (p. 73). Sometimes Watt's hypotheses collapse and he is forced to find others. Sometimes he finds that things change and he can go back to the original hypothesis.

Watt's main preoccupation is the nature of reality about which he has woolly ideas, and, more specifically, the nature of the supernatural, personified in Mr Knott, who is described in scriptural language: 'Watt had more and more the impression, as time passed, that nothing could be added to Mr Knott's establishment, and from it nothing taken away, but that as it was now, so it had been in the beginning, and so it would remain in the end' (p. 129). 'Nothing changed in Mr Knott's establishment, because nothing remained and nothing came or went, because all was a coming and a going' (p. 130). The narrator says tartly: 'Watt seemed highly pleased with this tenth-rate xenium'.

The three most important things that Watt discovers about Mr Knott are: first, that his slops had to be emptied 'before sunrise, or after sunset, on the violet bed in violet time, and on the pansy bed in pansy time, and on the rose bed in **rose** time' (p. 65); second, that when Watt gives up one of his **duties** – supervising the dog who eats Mr Knott's leftover food – 'which might have been supposed to have the gravest consequences . . . no punishment fell on Watt, no thunderbolt' (p. 113); and third (and Sam says that it is Watt's first surmise of any interest on the subject of Mr Knott) that Mr Knott 'needed a witness'. But, as Watt was 'an imperfect witness' and consequently 'witnessed ill', there was not much value in his surmise (p. 202).

Watt himself, however, is good for a certain amount of high comedy. Predictably, his love-life is an important focus. In *Watt*, once more, the imperfection of human love is used as a target for comedy, the tone throughout is mocking. The chief example in *Watt* is the much quoted episode of Watt's affair with Mrs Gorman, the fishwoman, who had had several admirers. We learn that Watt had had at least two well-defined romances, 'in the course of his celibate', and that he was 'not a man's man'. Mrs Gorman would call on Thursdays, and sit on Watt's knee drinking

stout. But Mrs Gorman did not always sit on Watt, for sometimes
Watt sat on Mrs Gorman. A page of permutations of these
positions follows, and the narrator slyly comments: 'Further than
this, it will be learned with regret, they never went, though more
than half inclined to do so on more than one occasion', because
'Watt had not the strength and Mrs Gorman had not the time
. . . . The irony of life! Of life in love! That he who has the time
should lack the force, and she who has the force should lack the
time!' This bawdy theme is sustained, with heightened comic
effect: 'if Watt had had a little more vigour, Mrs Gorman would
have just the time, and if Mrs Gorman had had a little more time
Watt could very likely have developed, with a careful nursing of
his languid tides, a breaker not unworthy of the occasion'
(pp. 140–1). There is a paragraph of repetitive trivia about what
drew them to each other suggesting that she, perhaps, was drawn
by a bottle of stout, he by the smell of fish. 'This was a view
towards which, in later years, when Mrs Gorman was no more
than a fading memory, than a dying perfume, Watt inclined.'

Something new in *Watt* is the lengthy development of the sick,
disgusting or cruel joke, for example the Lynch family diseases
(p. 98), the death of the dog O'Connor, the killing of birds. The
laugh here is not the distanced laugh at what is unhappy, but a
kick at God and the cruelty of existence. The diseases of the
Lynch family are so many and so awful that they become black
comedy. Set out in a list, they are a disaster, but the Lynch family
are concerned only with keeping up their numbers (in the hope of
hitting the thousand-year mark), and disease and decay do not
deter them. They have so far attained 882 years (though the
author informs us the figure is erroneous). As well as horror-
comedy there is satire here on the breeding habits of those who
should not breed, akin to Swift's 'A Modest Proposal'.

Still attacking the deity, the narrator tells us that it was in their
cruel acts that Watt and Sam 'came nearest to God', 'Robins in
particular, thanks to their confidingness, we destroyed in great
numbers' (p. 153). Here Beckett's intention is to shock, in order to
convey a strong image of the cruelty of the creator. His choice of a
universal favourite, the robin, emphasises the horror, and it
produces, as it is meant to, an outraged guffaw. Equally appalling,
and funny because it is an impossible feat, is Louit's treatment of
his dog O'Connor, which accompanies him on a research trip.
Caught in a bog, penniless and hungry, Louit holds O'Connor

head down in the bog 'until his faithful heart had ceased to beat', and roasts him in his skin which he could not bring himself to remove, over a fire of 'flags and cotton blossoms', flowery but non-combustible. This is heavily ironical. Louit had told the academic committee that he would not need a grant for O'Connor's subsistence as he 'would live off the land'; whereas it is he who has lived off O'Connor (p. 171).

In *Watt*, the digressions, already a familiar comic feature of *Murphy*, are elevated to extended and witty set pieces, and the anecdote about Louit is one of these. It is told by Arthur, to relieve the tedium of Mr Knott's establishment, 'the mysteries of which . . . Arthur had sometimes more than he could bear' (p. 199). Louit is a failed scholar (who ends up running the firm which produces the aphrodisiac, Bando). His dissertation is entitled 'The Mathematical Intuitions of the Visicelts', and, when he is interviewed by an academic committee, he produces an Irish labourer, Mr Nackybal, to whom he has taught the cube roots of a selected list of figures, and induces the committee to test the old man. Much nonsensical comedy is squeezed out of this situation. As for the non-verbal part of the comedy, there are six pages minutely describing the permutations of the ways in which the committee look at each other. Louit fails to convince them, and there are two pages of the ways in which they overtake each other as they are released at sunset from the meeting. 'And Louit, going down the stairs, met the bitter stout porter, Power, coming up' (p. 196), a flashback to Murphy's favourite joke. This story of the committee leaves the most profound impression on Watt of anything he saw or heard during his stay in Mr Knott's house, and it has poignancy, mirrored in the phrase: 'Rose and gloom, farewell and hail mingled, clashed, vanquished, victor vanquished, in the vast indifferent chamber' (p. 191), which gives a particularly strong bitter-sweet effect.

There is another long digression on Bando (perhaps from the French 'bander'), the aphrodisiac product which Louit later 'runs'. The impotent gardener, Mr Graves, is advised by Arthur to try Bando, in a comic send-up of advertising language, which after four years had changed him from being 'moody, listless, constipated' to 'a popular nudist, regular in my daily health, almost a father, and a lover of boiled potatoes'. 'The unfortunate thing about Bando', continues Arthur, 'is that it is no longer to be obtained in this unfortunate country. He adds that, smuggled in, 'it is immediately seized and confiscated by some gross customs official half-crazed with seminal intoxication' (linguistic joke). There are other, inconsequential digressions, for instance, Watt remembers lying in a ditch, when young, listening to the croaking of frogs, and there are two pages of variations on the theme krik, krak, krek (p. 135).

Watt's hallucinations are funny, and have little to do with the development of the narration, such as it is, or of what is happening, as far as it can be told. His 'voices' are often those of a mixed choir singing nonsense, or surrealistic 'threnes'; There is one about a bun:

> Oh a bun, a big fat bun
> For Mr Man and a bun
> For Mrs Man and a bun
> For Master Man and a bun
> for Miss Man and a bun
> a big fat bun
> for everyone.

We are told that Watt preferred the first voice: 'Bun is such a sad word, is it not? And man is not much better, is it?' (pp. 32–4). In another of Watt's hallucinations, a figure appears. He waits for it to draw near and set his mind at rest: 'He was not concerned with what the figure was in reality, but with what the figure appeared to be in reality. For since when were Watt's concerns with what things were, in reality?', reminding us that Watt is an absurd figure, in his opinion.

The characterisation in *Watt* is an important part of the comedy, and involves wit and wordplay. There is some light-hearted fun, for instance, about Mr Nolan the station-master, 'whose spirits always rose as he reached the station in the morning', and rose again, as he left in the evening: 'Thus Mr Nolan was assured, twice a day, of a rise in spirits.' Mr Nolan's other enjoyments are his meals and his newspaper. He is a great reader of the evening paper, five times a day, at his tea, at his supper, at his breakfast, with his morning stout, and at his dinner. He has a 'gallant nature', for when he had thoroughly read the penny newspaper he would place it in the 'ladies house of office', for the convenience of the ladies. The narrator, playing on the 'spending a penny' theme, comments, 'few pennyworths give more joy than Mr Nolan's evening paper' (p. 237).

More serious characters who inspire wit and irony are Arsene and Arthur, who, like Watt, are servants and witnesses of Mr Knott. Arsene is a better witness than Watt. He takes a very black view of existence, which is 'to hunger, thirst, lust every day afresh and every day in vain', and considers that humanity is not fit to exercise will-power and should be forcibly restrained. He thinks those who are happy are those held back from their vices: 'the glutton castaway, the drunkard in the desert, the lecher in prison' (p. 43), because it is man's own weakness which betrays him. Yet, Arsene acknowledges that it is useless not to seek, not to want because it is the nearest we get to felicity. Deeply aware of the paradoxical nature of existence, and that its experiences are universal, Arsene says that personally he regrets everything, good and bad. For Arsene there is: 'not a word not a deed, not a thought, not a need, not a grief, not a joy, not a girl, not a boy, not a doubt, not a trust, not a scorn, not a lust, not a hope, not a fear, not a smile, not a tear, not a name, not a face, no time, no place, that I do not regret exceedingly'.

Arthur, yet another of Mr Knott's servants and witnesses, takes a different attitude. He is a small fat clown, author of the stories of Louit and Bando, which he told to relieve the tensions of existence in Mr Knott's establishment, and which so entranced Watt. In the Addenda there is an anecdote about Arthur which illustrates his sense of fun. Laughing heartily at an aphorism he 'was obliged to lean for support against a passing shrub, or bush, which joined heartily in the joke. When he had recovered his calm, he turned to examine the bush, or shrub. All he could say was that it was not a rush' (Addenda to *Watt*, p. 253). (Wordplay on *roseau pensant* perhaps.) In the garden he meets an old man, who says he helped to lay out the 'darling place'. 'In that case', said Arthur, 'perhaps you can tell me the name of this extraordinary growth.' 'That's what we calls a hardy laurel', said the old man (more wordplay, on Laurel and Hardy). Arthur went back into the house and wrote in his journal: 'Took a turn in the garden. Made merry with the hardy laurel' (p. 253). Such nonsense dialogue and action is an important aspect of *Watt*, especially at the end of the book. Often the dialogue or action is close to that of Lewis Carroll, for instance the conversation of the piano tuners,

the Galls, about the piano damaged by mice, or, in the episode
when Watt purchases a railway ticket after leaving Mr Knott's
house (p. 244):

> Where to? said Mr Nolan
> To the end of the line, said Watt . . .
> Which end? said Mr Nolan
> Watt did not reply.
> The round end, or the square end? said Mr Nolan.
> Watt reflected a little longer. Then he said The nearer end.
> The nearest end, cried Mr Nolan. . . .
> I beg your pardon, said Watt, I mean the farther end. (p. 244)

As for the action, the book ends dramatically on a nonsensical
note with the disappearance, apparently into thin air, of Watt
(like the Baker in Lewis Carroll's *Hunting of the Snark*, who 'softly
and suddenly vanished away'),[14] and a paragraph follows of looks
at each other by the three baffled railwaymen, a comic reprise of
the academic committee's looks at each other earlier. In this kind
of non-verbal comedy *Watt* looks forward to the non-verbal
comedy of the plays, particularly *Waiting for Godot*.

Language is often used purely as comedy. There are the comic
paradoxes of 'the brightening trouble', 'the forgotten horrors of
joy' uttered by Sam and Arsene. There is the schoolboy comedy
'cute of the roob' for root of the cube, or 'pissabed' for dandelion.
There is the humour of bathetic statements, Sam refers poetically
to 'the night that covers all things with its cloak', and adds:
'Especially when the weather is cloudy' (p. 214). Or, in the
Addenda: 'The sky was of a dark colour from which it may be
inferred that the usual luminaries were absent. They were', or 'Mr
Case carried a storm lantern in his hand. From it issued a yellow
beam of extraordinary debility' (p. 332). There is the absurd:
Watt's block hat was once 'mustard, now it was pepper in colour'
(p. 217). But the best example of the felicity of comic language is
expressed by Sam in the passage about Irish Mr Graves's
pronunciation of third and fourth as turd and fart. 'Watt liked
these venerable Saxon words . . . when Mr Graves drinking his
afternoon stout said, 'Tis only me turd or fart, then Watt felt he
was prostituting himself for some purpose' (p. 142).

The weaknesses of language are particularly expressed in Watt's
seven modes of muddled reportage on Mr Knott, which is close to

Jabberwocky, and has a serious function. The breakdown of language illustrates Watt's gradual breakdown under the stress of serving Mr Knott and his establishment. Possibly it is an attempt at the 'hermetic language' mentioned in the Surrealist Manifesto signed by Beckett, among others, in *transition* (March 1932, pp. 148–9) which states: 'The final disintegration of the "I" in the creative act is made possible by the use of language which is a mantic instrument and which does not hesitate to adopt a revolutionary attitude towards words and syntax, going even so far as to invent a hermetic language if necessary.' Although such nonsense language has a comic or inconsequential effect it is at the same time an important illustration of the process of the breakdown of language, which indicates Beckett's growing dissatisfaction with words as a means of expression. The main and very serious issue raised in *Watt* is the impossibility of real communication, and it heralds the much more serious treatment of this theme in *The Unnamable*. Maybe as a trial solution of this problem, Beckett turned to writing in French, as a means of saying what he had to say. Inevitably, this led to new forms of word play, and to gallic as well as gallows humour.

5

First Steps in French

The period after *Watt*, written in hiding during the Occupation, was a turning point in Beckett's career as a writer. On his return to Paris, he began to write in French, commencing in 1945 with the nostalgic 'Premier Amour', followed by the bitter 'L'Expulsé', 'La Fin' and 'Le Calmant'. He has described these novellas as 'four phases of one existence'.[1]

The narration of the novellas, ambiguous, often incongruous, contains lewd and obscene detail. The tone is cool, neutral and ironical, and records the gradual decay of an unprepossessing character who, like Watt, is persecuted, but bears no ill-will towards his persecutors, accepting the status of outcast of society and looking on existence as a bad dream which, annoyingly for him, paradoxically contains hints of better things. The hero consoles himself in this half-life by telling himself stories, which do not satisfy him: 'I don't know why I told this story', he says, 'I could just as well have told another.' The paradoxical nature of existence comes over strongly in the novellas. Talking of his pains in 'First Love' he says: 'But even them, my pains, I understand ill. That must come from my not being all pain and nothing else. There's the rub . . . . To be nothing but pain, how that would simplify matters' (*Four Novellas*, p. 17).

'First Love' is bitterly ironical, peppered with obscenities, and ruefully nostalgic. It was not published until 1970 'because the woman who had inspired it was still alive'.[2] Like Watt's story it begins with locked doors but this time there is no admittance. At twenty-five, the narrator is shut out, by the death of his father, from the protected world of childhood and this results in his 'marriage', to secure a refuge. The title is cruelly ironical. *First Love*, with its echoes of *Murphy*, is about the narrator's exploitation of a kind-hearted prostitute who gives him a home. Here Beckett makes bitter attacks on 'love', but his raillery is not without humour. As far as comedy is concerned, this is the funniest of the novellas. *First Love* begins with a two-and-a-half page digression, a macabre soliloquy on cemeteries, beginning: 'Personally I have no bone to pick with graveyards'. He enjoys picnicking in them, his sandwich, or banana taste sweeter when he is sitting on a tomb. He likes to wander among the slabs, 'culling the inscriptions'. 'Of these', he says, 'I never weary, there are always three or four of such drollery that I have to hold on to the cross, or the stele, or the angel, so as not to fall.' He also likes to muse on his own epitaph: 'My other writings are no sooner dry than they revolt me, but my epitaph still meets with my approval.' He comments pedantically on its style: 'the second and last or rather latter line limps a little', he says, 'but that is no great matter' (p. 11). In cemeteries 'with a little luck', he says, 'you hit on a genuine interment with real live mourners' (to contrast with the dead) . . . 'and nearly always that charming business with the dust'. He thinks it unlikely that there would be anything powdery about the deceased 'unless he happed to have died, or she, by fire' but concedes: 'their little gimmick with the dust is charming' (p. 11).

At this point, he remembers his readers' expectations of a love story, and briskly remarks: 'But, to pass to less melancholy matters . . .', only to recount that the death of his father had caused him to be thrown out of his home. In his lifetime his father always said, 'let him stay', when the family wanted to get rid of him. He says that they succeeded in locking him out of his room while he was in the lavatory, which evokes a perennial joke of Beckett's, constipation: 'It was, I am now convinced anxiety constipation. But was I genuinely constipated? Somehow I think not. Softly, softly', followed by another lavatory joke, a picture of Jesus and his flock, 'presiding' over his efforts (p. 16). He ends by telling us it is all a muddle in his head: 'graves and nuptials and the different varieties of motion', another lavatory joke. Then he decides again to pass on to less melancholy matters, and the love story can begin (p. 19). It is short but not sweet, and is comic in tone.

Her name was Lulu, and they met on the bank of the canal where he was watching the stars; which is reminiscent of the meeting of Celia and Murphy. He was lying on his favourite hidden bench: 'Shove up', she says. She wanted to sit down, and his 'first movement was to go, but my fatigue and my having nowhere to go, dissuaded me from acting on it' (p. 21). Lulu sings quietly to herself and he enjoys it: 'The voice, though out of tune, was not unpleasant. It breathed of a soul too soon wearied ever to conclude', which he describes as 'that perhaps least arse-aching soul of all' (p. 21), high praise from a Beckett hero. Soon Lulu's company attracts him, and he looks out for her. Their relationship deepens to the extent that he rests his feet in her lap and she strokes his ankles. This is funny for the reader, but destructive for him, because its effect is to disturb the 'supineness in the mind, the dulling of the self', which is his preferred state.

The idea of love he finds unattractive, for he considers that 'What goes by the name of love is banishment, with now and then a postcard from the homeland'. 'Such is my considered opinion', he continues pedantically. He didn't understand women at that period, he says, adding, nor men either, nor animals either; what he really understood was limited to his own pains, which he enjoyed thinking of: 'those of the mind, those of the heart or emotional conative, those of the soul (none prettier than these) and finally those of the frame proper'. He likes to consider the latter, from head to foot 'beloved of the corn, the cramp, the kibe, the bunion, the hammer toe, the nail ingrown, the fallen arch, the common blain, the club foot, duck foot, goose foot, pigeon foot, flat foot, trench foot and other curiosities' (p. 28). The macabre humour of this list is heightened by the reader's consciousness that preoccupation with such conditions has nothing to do with love.

He senses this, because he returns to the subject of his love story, such as it is. As autumn approached the trysting place became unsuitable as 'the air was beginning to strike chill, and for other reasons', he informs the reader, 'better not wasted on cunts like you' (p. 29). He finds another refuge in a deserted cowshed where he writes Lulu's name on the dried cowpats because: 'For the first time in my life . . . I had to contend with a feeling which gradually assumed, to my dismay, the dread name of love'. He thinks it is love because he had 'heard of the thing at home, in school, in brothel and at church, and had read romances in prose and verse under the guidance of my tutor, in six or seven languages, both dead and living' (p. 31). To assuage his pain he tears up nettles, though he comments that he was not himself; 'it's not like me, to do that to weeds, on the contrary, I'd smother them in manure if I had any. Flowers are a different matter. Love brings out the worst in men and no error' (p. 32). An intellectual discussion follows of what kind of love possesses him. He rejects love-passion, 'the priapic one'; there are so many varieties of love, he says, adding ironically 'all equally if not more delicious, are there not?'. It is not, he thinks, Platonic, disinterested love, but he sums up: 'My thoughts were all of Lulu, if that doesn't give you some idea nothing will'. Here, he announces that he is sick and tired of the name Lulu and will change it to Anna. He says he thinks of her 'twenty minutes, twenty-five minutes and even as long as half an hour daily', concluding: 'That must have been my way of loving' (p. 34).

In December or January, when, he quips, 'the cold was seasonable, that is to say reasonable, like all that is seasonable', he returns to the bench. She is there and he asks her why she is pursuing him, a farcical touch. Lulu/Anna is wearing a muff, the sight of which brings tears to his eyes. He says: 'And yet I felt no sorrow. When I found myself in tears for no apparent reason it meant I had caught sight of something unbeknownst' (p. 37). Something, he says, if not the muff, had 'unmanned' him. He longs to be gone, but asks her to sing and she does so, about lemon or orange trees, he cannot remember which. This provokes a long unpunctuated digression on the impossibility of getting through the world without hearing singing, a digression which finishes abruptly with: 'this sentence has gone on long enough'.

He tears himself away but is drawn back by doubts as to whether she has finished singing, which prefigures the end of the story when he runs away from the noises of childbirth. He says: 'To have to harbour such a doubt was something I preferred to avoid at that period. I lived of course in doubt, on doubt, but such trivial doubts as this, purely somatic as some say, were best cleared up without delay, they could nag at me like gnats for weeks on end' (p. 40): an illuminating statement of his point of view. Divided like Murphy, intellectual doubts were his life, but trivial day-to-day ones, of the body, must be disposed of. So he returns to the bench and Lulu reappears at last. He takes her arm to see whether it gives him pleasure: 'it gave me none, I let her go'. She looks neither young nor old. Such ambiguity, he says, 'I found difficult to bear at that period' (p. 42).

When Anna/Lulu says she has a room, he asks rhetorically: 'Who has not a room?', adding, 'Ah, I hear the clamour'. She has two rooms and a kitchen, she adds. This he describes as 'At last conversation worthy of the name', and decides to move in. Though he does not feel at ease with her, he feels he would be 'at least free to think of something else than her, of the old trusty things, and so, little by little, as down steps towards a deep, of nothing. And I knew that away from her I would forfeit this freedom' (p. 44). When they reach her home, truly professional, she immediately undresses. This of course was not what he had come for, though he says: 'Fortunately she was not the first naked woman to have crossed my path . . . I knew she would not explode' (p. 95). This is a comic interlude: he interrupts her with a request to see the other room, and she has to put on a wrap to show him the way. He throws out the furniture, excepting the sofa which he turns to the wall, and climbs into this refuge 'like a dog into its basket'. 'Already my love was waning, that was all that mattered', he says, 'Yes, already I felt better, soon I'd be up to the slow descent again, the long submersions, so long denied me through her fault' (p. 51).

His feeling of reassurance is short-lived, he thought he was all set for a good night in spite of the strange surroundings, but, in a reversal of roles, she seduces him as he sleeps. He exclaims pathetically: 'I woke next morning quite worn out . . . . One shudders to think of her exertions . . .', concluding fatuously, 'It was my night of love' (p. 53). Anna/Lulu leaves him alone after this, but the sound of her clients, he says, annoyed him: 'I couldn't make out if it was always the same gent or more than one. Lovers' groans are so alike, and lovers' giggles.' He taxes her, 'So you live by prostitution', and she says with dignity, 'We live by prostitution' (p. 56). She puts up curtains between their rooms to lessen the sounds and they settle to a curious domesticity, as she becomes more a landlady than a lover. One day he orders parsnips, telling us in a comic digression: 'I like parsnips because they taste like violets and violets because they smell like parsnips. Were there no parsnips on earth violets would leave me cold, and if violets did not exist I would care as little for parsnips as I do for turnips, or radishes. And even in the present state of our flora, I mean on this planet where parsnips and violets contrive to co-exist, I could do without both with the utmost ease, the uttermost ease' (p. 57).

The days go by, then Anna/Lulu tells him she is 'with child'. 'Perhaps it's just wind', he answers, then advises her to 'Abort, abort . . .'. When she says she can feel it 'lepping already', he cries 'If it's lepping it's not mine' (p. 59). Things, he says, 'went from bad to worse, to worse and worse'. He considers leaving, but is prudent, 'I might have been worse off than I was in that house . . . it fell short of my ideal naturally, but I wasn't blind to its advantages . . .'. In spite of these advantages however he decides to go. What finished him, he points out, was the birth: 'It woke me up'. He cannot stand the cries; though, typically, he sympathises, not with Anna/Lulu, but with the newborn. 'What that infant must have been going through', he muses. He is consoled by gazing at the stars and remembering his father who first showed them to him, thus returning to infancy. This is the end of 'love', he remarks: 'I could have done with other loves perhaps. But there it is, either you love or you don't.'

The next work in the series (taking them in order of writing) is *Mercier and Camier* in which a more positive note is struck in its many recommendations of 'a sense of proportion', an important step on the quest for the *risus purus*. Completed in 1946 – and not published until 1970 – *Mercier and Camier* is based on an unfinished work: *Les Bosquets de Bondy* (Den of Thieves).[3] The lone hero of the previous works now gives way to the couple, one short, one tall and closely interdependent, closely related to Vladimir and Estragon of *Waiting for Godot*. They share the same questionable quest: 'Did what they were looking for exist? Did they know what they were looking for?' The dialogue, too, heralds that of *Waiting for Godot*; it is a way of passing time. It is this and their companionship that provides a kind of certainty in an uncertain world, though this companionship has its drawbacks: 'Admittedly strength was needed for to stay with Camier, no less than for to stay with Mercier, but less than for the horrors of soliloquy' (p. 78).

The Narrator, who accompanies them on their journey, comments here – reinforcing the argument for companionship as a positive help in the uncertainties of existence – that although generally speaking Mercier was the live wire, Camier the dead weight:

> The reverse was to be expected at any moment. On the less weak let the weaker always lean, for the course to follow. They might conceivably be valiant together. That would be the day. Or the great weakness might overtake them simultaneously. Let them in this case not give way to despair, but wait with confidence for the evil moment to pass. (p. 19)

Mercier and Camier is the most dramatic of the novels, and more important, it is the first of Beckett's works consciously to juxtapose the paradoxes of existence, good and evil, negation and affirmation, tragedy and comedy. Before Mercier and Camier begin their quest, he says:

> They had consulted together at length, before embarking on this journey, weighing with all the calm at their command what benefits they might hope from it, what ills apprehend, maintaining turn about the dark side and the rosy. (pp. 7–8)

This is a key sentence because, throughout the book, Mercier and Camier try to keep this balance, which will produce what Mercier calls 'a sense of proportion', the attainment of which is so necessary to being able to laugh at what is unhappy, the *risus purus*.

This book, like so much of Beckett's work, is a vehicle for satire on the human condition and human fallibility, man's lot being seen as nasty, brutish and too long, and deprivation the natural course of events. The countryside, almost certainly Irish, is described as 'quickset hedgerows, mud, liquid manure, ricks, wallows, cowshit, hovels, and here and there a form unmistakably human scratching at his plot since the first scabs of dawn or shifting his dung, with a spade, having lost his shovel and his fork, being broken' (p. 106). This scene, and the Irish peasant, is possibly the source of all Beckett's deprived heroes: his graceless existence a preview of theirs.

In a very black passage, life is likened to trash in the pocket of an abandoned raincoat, a mixture of:

> Punched tickets, of all sorts, spent matches, scraps of newspaper bearing in their margins the obliterated traces of irrevocable rendez-vous, the classic last tenth of pointless pencil, crumples of soiled bumf, a few porous condoms. Life in short.

'Nothing we'll be needing?', says Mercier, 'Did you not hear what I said?', replies Camier, 'Life' (p. 66). Nature, too, is far from kind. But it is man's inhumanity to man that inspires the most scathing comment: 'Our brethren are there to dispel our hopes.'

Man's cruelty and social divisiveness inspire the blackest irony, and the social outcast is likened to a hunted animal. The narrator enlarges on this: 'Yes, when you outrage nature you need to be mighty careful if you don't want to hear a view-halloo . . .'

(p. 81), a colourful image of the chase, with a man as the quarry. He is similarly caustic in a passage drawing attention to the difference between the haves and have-nots, contrasting the situation of Mercier and Camier, homeless in a dark alley, with that of the complacent inmates of the homes around them, drowsing and enjoying the sound of wind and rain lashing the panes, as their thoughts idly turn to those outside who have no refuge: 'the unable, the accursed, the weak, the unfortunate' (p. 86).

However, the general tone of *Mercier and Camier* is as light as that of *Murphy*, and the dark side of existence is balanced by a comic view. This juxtaposition of pathos and humour is the leitmotif of the novel, which provides a gloss on the later, more obscure, *Waiting for Godot*. The black side is there, of course; for instance, the murder of the policeman. But it is not over-emphasised in this novel. Mercier's imagination also inspires dark passages; he is troubled, for example, by his meeting with the old man with the donkey (a character from the novella 'The End'), and especially, like Watt, by imaginary voices. The narrator tells us that the least thing halts the Merciers of this world; 'a murmur coming to its crest and breaking, a voice saying how strange the autumn-tide of day no matter what the season' (p. 76) but these voices cease at last, and the narrator reassures us, Mercier will recover, ready to start off again, 'his being filled with that merciful fog which is the best he knows'.

Comic passages are numerous throughout the book, which, like *Murphy*, sets the scene and tone from the beginning. It is morning: 'On all hands already the workers were at it again, the air waxed loud with cries of pleasure and pain and with the urbaner notes of those for whom life had exhausted its surprises, as well on the minus side as on the plus' (p. 12). Such passages combine word-play and paradox, with devastating effect. Daily habits are derided as too tedious to enumerate, though some are attempted: 'getting up, dressing up (paramount), ingesting, excreting, undressing up, dossing down' (p. 108) and we are told, with heavy irony, that there is no danger of losing interest under these conditions: 'You cultivate your memory, till it's passable, a treasure bin, stroll in your crypt, unlit, return to the scenes, call back the old sounds (paramount) . . .' (p. 108). Thus, memory is a garbage can, we live in a charnel house.

Much of the humour of *Mercier and Camier* comes from the

narrator's interpolations. When dates are given, and the reader is working out the ages of the two heroes, he intervenes (p. 16): 'Conclude nothing from these idle words, Mercier and Camier were old young'. Or, about a character who will not be long on stage, but whose appearance is painstakingly described, he remarks: 'Some are best limned at first sight, those liable to vanish and never reappear'.

The threesome, Mercier, Camier and Watt, inspires authorial witticisms. Doubtless thinking of the three musketeers, Watt says it is a pity Dumas the Elder cannot see them. 'Or one of the evangelists', offers Camier, seeing them as the Trinity. The narrator interrupts here with the remark: 'A different class Mercier and Camier, for all their faults' (p. 112). When Mercier and Camier go off somewhere together, the narrator remarks: 'They advanced into the sunset', adding 'You can't deny yourself everything' (p. 112).

Mercier and Camier are clown characters, and from their improvisations comes much risqué or inconsequential comedy. When they break their journey in a pub, we are given the gist of their drunken exchanges, when 'a great light bathed their understandings, flooding in particular on the following concepts'. There are thirteen of these 'concepts' including money, bicycles, needs, life, intuition, soul ('another four letter word'), God, the problem of being without women ('exploring other channels'). We are told that it is in bars that the Merciers and Camiers find it least tedious to await the dark.

The journey of Mercier and Camier can be seen as an allegory of human existence and its attendant chances and changes, of which an individual lifetime is only a small part, as man himself is a small part, temporally and spatially, of a vast enterprise. Though the purpose of the journey is unknown, it is implied that there is more to it than merely keeping on the move. Nevertheless, keeping on the move is important in this haphazard progress toward the unknown, and their watchword is suitable: 'Lente, lente, and circumspection, with deviations to right and left and sudden reversals of course. . . . We have all life before us, all the fag end that is' (p. 67). The most important element in their journey through a life-time is their endless dialogue. Camier is disposed to question accidents like the loss of their possessions (the sack, the umbrella). Mercier advises him to ask fewer questions, to take things as they come, but Camier does not agree with this. Mercier says: 'Shall we fritter away what little is left of us in the tedium of flight and dreams of deliverance? Do you not inkle, like me, how you might adjust yourself to this preposterous penalty and placidly await the executioner, come to ratify you? No, said Camier' (p. 89).

Mercier himself has given up asking questions and 'hasn't an answer' to his name: 'Oh there was a time I had, and none but the best, they were my only company . . . . But I sent them packing long ago' (p. 87). Mercier, the thinking man, remains passive, he 'bows to the irrecusable, a habit one contracts among the axioms' (p. 106). The less thoughtful Camier questions providence, though he agrees about the practical advantage of adapting to changes. Where the meditative Mercier submits philosophically to the workings of fate, the pragmatic Camier looks on it as a challenge, and between them, they strike a balance.

In *Mercier and Camier*, the divided personality of a Murphy, or of a Belacqua, is transformed into two personalities, each with his own attitudes and opinions. This results in dialectic on universal issues, a double view rather than a soliloquy, sometimes inconsequential, always open-ended. Such dialogue, with its mixture of sense and nonsense, looks forward to the drama.

Devoted to each other, as Vladimir and Estragon are, Mercier and Camier squabble, yet remain together, for they have a common aim. The heroes of *Waiting for Godot* also have a common aim, to wait for Godot. But Mercier and Camier share an urge to keep moving, exploring possibilities:

> I see different lands, said Mercier.
> Where are we going? said Camier.
> Shall I never shake you off? said Mercier.
> Do you not know where we are going? said Camier.
> What does it matter, said Mercier, where we are going? We are going, that's enough. (p. 90)

This concept too, is important in *Waiting for Godot*. As the goal is undefined, when Camier asks in which direction, Mercier merely replies, 'Crooked ahead' (p. 185). The couple are almost inseparable. After they have been parted for a while and are reunited, Camier cries, 'There you are at last. I thought you had left me forever', which is later echoed, in *Waiting for Godot*, by

Estragon. Their humour, too, is similar to that of Vladimir and Estragon: travelling through a bog they are exhausted and near to collapse. They decide to rest in a ruined house and make a joke combining the words 'collapse' and 'ruin'. Mercier and Camier, like Vladimir and Estragon, see their fate as predetermined, a story merely to be acted out. Mercier says, 'We are fraught with more events than could fit in a fat tome, two fat tomes, your fat tome and my fat tome. Whence no doubt our blessed sense of nothing, nothing to be done, nothing to be said' (p. 87). This latter remark, 'Nothing to be done', echoes later as the opening speech of *Waiting for Godot*.

There are other similarities between this novel and the play, for instance the appointments. The action begins in *Mercier and Camier* with a comic passage explaining how Mercier and Camier just missed each other, when first one, and then the other, arrived at the appointed place, but not at the same time, and left to seek the other. At the end of this passage the narrator says: 'What stink of artifice'. Even nearer to the atmosphere of the appointment with Godot is Mr Conaire's appointment with Camier, when Mr Conaire says: 'You appointed to meet me here, at this very place . . . I arrive . . . I wait. Doubts assail me. Can I have mistaken the place? The day? The hour?' (p. 62). There is the same comic anxiety about the ambiguity of appointments, in both the novel and the play, the same doubts, about place, day, hour. Later Camier says to Mercier that he was on the point of not keeping 'our appointment', and the narrator ejaculates, 'So they had an appointment' (p. 91), as if the characters had taken over, and had done something he did not know about.

There is in *Mercier and Camier* the sense of opposites, the contradictions of existence, the juxtaposition of pathos and comedy and the determination to keep trying, which is also an important feature of *Waiting for Godot*. It is exemplified in this exchange:

If we have nothing to say, said Camier, let us say nothing.
We have things to say, said Mercier.
Then why don't we say them? said Camier.
We can't, said Mercier.
Then let us be silent, said Camier.
But we try, said Mercier. (p. 86)

In *Mercier and Camier*, as in *Waiting for Godot*, the notion of
going on trying is as important as the balance between laughter
and tears. Mercier recommends Camier to acquire a sense of
proportion: 'When you fear for your cyst think of your fistula.
And when you tremble for your fistula consider your chancre.
This method holds equally for what is called happiness' (p. 58). A
sense of proportion, he implies, gives, if not freedom from
anxiety, a standpoint from which it can be controlled. What he is
aiming at is the frame of mind which can be ruffled neither by
good fortune nor bad. To support this argument Mercier takes as
an example 'un type' (translated into English as 'one') who has
nothing, who is deprived mentally and physically. He asks where
such an individual can turn for relief, and answers with devastating
humour, 'Nothing simpler, to the thought of annihilation. Thus
whatever the conjuncture nature bids us smile, if not laugh'
(p. 58). The couple are amused by this sally: 'Camier began to
laugh. Mercier in due course was tickled too. Then they laughed
long together, clutching at each other by the shoulders so as not
to collapse. "What innocent merriment," said Camier finally.'
Such black comedy *is* innocent, and preserves a free attitude to
the assaults of providence. In distancing themselves they are on
the way to the *risus purus* which laughs at fate. Because they seek
a 'sense of proportion' their quest and conversations are valuable
because they make possible their survival as individuals.

Mercier and Camier, it is true, are hardly 'valiant together', but
after many journeys and shared troubles, they can hold their own
against the negativism of Watt, whom they meet in the last chapter.
Watt 'knew them in their cradles', he knew Murphy, too, who
was younger, 'less battered', than they are. In the pub he tries to
get them down. Mercier and Camier 'paid scant heed to these
sayings'. They do not agree with such sentiments, but are
overjoyed to see each other after an absence. Watt's defeatist
attitudes are not for them, and they reject him.

Walking by the canal they recall their life together, trying to see
where they went wrong. 'Looking back on it', said Camier, 'we
heard ourselves speaking of everything but ourselves.' 'We didn't
bring it off', said Mercier, 'I grant you that.' He takes thought and
adds: 'Perhaps we might . . .'. It is possible he means 'might
bring it off if we tried again'. They go to look at Mercier's
'prospect' over the canal, which, visionary as he is, he calls the
Ancient's Blessed Isles. 'They weren't hard to please', muses the

more down-to-earth Camier. 'You wait', said Mercier, 'You only barely saw, but you'll never forget . . . . You'll be back.' The narrator indicates that it is inspiration, companionship, moments of hope like this, that, in spite of disasters, are 'Enough to tempt you, joking apart, to have another go . . .' (p. 108).

'Having another go' resulted, in 1947, in a division of effort, the composition concurrently of the dark-toned and pessimistic *Molloy*, and, 'to relieve myself of the awful depression the prose led me into', the play, *Eleuthéria*. 'Life at that time was too demanding, too terrible, and I thought theatre would be a diversion.[4] *Eleuthéria* – the noble Greek title, Freedom, is juxtaposed by the sub-title 'Drame bourgeois' – is about the impossibility of achieving freedom, and the need to continue to seek it by staying outside society. It is also about the impossibility of putting into words any abstract, yet vital notion, in this case liberty. Because it treats a serious concept in a throwaway fashion, the play has an important part in the series, as it illustrates Beckett's sly method of presenting his views obliquely, without commitment.

Freedom is important throughout Beckett's works. As early as *Murphy* he coined a word to describe a peat fire which 'Irish in its eleutheromania, would not burn behind bars' (p. 75). Beckett wrote to George Reavey in 1947 announcing that he had finished a play in three acts: 'Eleuthéromane, I'm not quite sure'.[5] Again, writing to Reavey, he described it as 'part of the series; *Watt*, *Mercier and Camier*, *Molloy*, not to mention the four Nouvelles and Eleuthéria.[6] This play, although it has not been performed, is not one of the works which Beckett kept under wraps. In August he wrote that it had been 'almost published, but only almost'.[7] In the spring of 1950 he offered it to Roger Blin, together with *Waiting for Godot*. Blin had worked with Artaud and at that time he was producing Strindberg's *Ghost Sonata* at the Gaieté-Montparnasse theatre. He thought Eleuthéria was interesting and would have produced it if theatre funds could have afforded the elaborate set and seventeen characters.

The play is Pirandellian in its unconventionality and interruptions of the action by characters like the Glazier, who acts as commentator, or the member of the audience who adds his own point of view to the debates on stage. The first half is conventional, almost banal, parodying the structure of a 'well-made play', and imitating the tone of the bourgeois theatre of the period. In contrast, and here lie the shock tactics and the comedy, the second half takes on the lightness, pace and anarchical humour of a play by Pirandello. The style of the first half enhances the second, in which the ideal of liberty is discussed. Or, on a more human level, the idea of 'live and let live' is suggested in the, usually passive, Victor's stirring exhortation to those on stage, and to the audience, to look critically at their own life style, rather than his. A key passage is the exchange between the member of the audience and Victor. The member of the audience tells Victor that it is *his* case which interests them, not the universal one of mankind. Victor replies, 'But they are the same thing' (Ils sont solidaires).

The play opens in the Krap salon, with a send-up of typical Parisian female conversation of the period, between Madame Krap, Victor's mother, her sister, Madame Piouk and Madame Meck, who are paying a call on her. Their names indicate their comic status and they use a period idiom, in a conventional and macabre exchange about their health, and the renegade Victor, who spends his time in bed or rifling dustbins.

With the arrival of their male counterparts there is some scatological tilting at literature and the human condition, and the tone is comically pedantic. Monsieur Krap, Victor's father, is one of Beckett's writer-characters who has some unkind things to say about literature, which he has given up. On the other hand, Dr Piouk 'interests' himself in 'humanity', which Mme Krap describes as a thorny problem. Dr Piouk considers himself a practical person and says in a Swiftian passage that he would solve this problem by banishing reproduction; among other things by beating reproductive women to death. He says he does not claim originality, but 'c'est une question d'organisation'. Yet, paradoxically, he would like an heir to whom he could 'pass on the torch'. Excited by this passage, Mme Krap offers to discuss with him her 'bas-ventre' over dinner, and he begs her not to do so before the cheese.

The second act takes place in Victor's sordid room. Victor tries to address the audience, fails and breaks a window, at which moment, the Glazier enters. The Glazier is no mere glazier but takes the part of the Greek chorus. He has no patience with Victor's high-falutin speeches about 'freedom' and asks him not to talk nonsense. They are interrupted by Mme Meck, Mlle Skunk, Victor's fiancée, and Dr and Mrs Piouk. As they enter they are tripped up by the Glazier, 'to amuse the gawpers', he says. Dr Piouk diagnoses Victor's malaise as 'consciousness' which he says should be suppressed, and offers Victor poison.

In Act 3 the Glazier asks Victor why he lives in this way. Victor says it is not easy to explain – 'un peu comme la musique'. An enraged member of the audience climbs on stage and politely excuses himself for the intrusion, but goes on more aggressively to say that he represents the audience who are protesting at the fatuity of the play. The landlady enters and says she has had enough. The Glazier says she is not the only one and the member of the audience agrees: 'we are all fed up with seeing you floating about like leaves in the wind'. The farce, he says, has gone on long enough: 'I say "farce" on purpose. It is what the best writers do. They give their serious works this description in case they are not taken seriously.' It is clear that this is a key passage, which underlines Beckett's claim that the most serious things are the funniest, echoed in *Endgame*, when Nell makes her important statement that there is nothing so comical as unhappiness.

The member of the audience falters in his argument: 'It's strange, I've only just joined you on stage and I begin to lose my place . . . everything becomes dim and I can't see clearly.' A voice from the *loge* reminds him that the farce has gone on long enough: 'La farce, la farce. Assez dureé'. Then the prompter joins in, climbing on stage, text in hand: 'That's enough. You're not following the text. I'm going home. Goodnight'. (He leaves.) The member of the audience agrees. The play paralyses and stupefies him, it is like watching an inexpert game of chess: 'you are wearied by its stupidity till in the end you can't hang on any longer and have to tell the players how to finish so everyone can go home to bed'. However, in an attempt to sort out the muddle he makes a pedantic speech beginning: 'Once again, I will be brief. I distinguish in all this hoo-ha two opposing attitudes'. One is Victor's, which he does not know how to describe (but suggests 'moral, aesthetic, intellectual, sensibility'), because his terms of reference are vague and intertwined. The other view is Dr Piouk's, which is much simpler: 'He seems to believe people turn from unhappiness as a butterfly from the shadows'. He says man's nature is naturally ambivalent; they are not really opposing attitudes, but co-exist: 'if you call that existence'. He then asks who wrote the play: 'Qui a fait ce navet' (literally turnip), and peers at his programme – Beckett (he says Becquet), Samuel Becquet – 'he must be a Greenland Jew crossed with an

Auvergnat'. The member-of-the-audience considers that he could have made something out of the two principles, duty and pleasure, and the unfortunate Victor, who cared for neither, and looked for something else. 'Then', he says, 'we might have enjoyed the play'. 'Listen', he continues, 'stop talking about what doesn't exist and see things as they are'. All this seems very reasonable and hopes are raised that the play will end in some kind of order.

The member-of-the-audience asks for one last effort. They have established that what Victor fears is unhappiness, but think maybe he lied. They call from the *loge* a stage Chinaman with torture instruments, and tell Victor unless he explains why he leads such an existence, they will tear out his fingernails. Victor says he will try, makes a false start at which the Spectateur snaps: 'Stick to the question', and Victor tries again. This again is a key speech, aimed at making the audience search their own consciences and conventional attitudes. He says, 'You find my way of life sordid and incomprehensible but you should take a good look at your own. Ask yourselves questions. What is it to you, the way I live?' The Glazier tells him that people are provoked by it, and want to understand. Victor asks: 'why this sudden fury to understand a life like mine. You are surrounded every day by numberless mysteries and remain indifferent, yet my case arouses your vulgar curiosity and you want to get to the bottom of it. Saints, fools, martyrs, leave you cold and you turn away.' The member of the audience tells Victor it is his case that interests them, not that of humankind, and Victor replies: 'but they are the same thing'. The member of the audience says it is now eleven o'clock and he doesn't care about Victor's existence, which is eroded by its liberty, not worth having. The Glazier suggests they should kill Victor and be done with it. The member of the audience says: 'let's be patient a bit longer', and asks Victor to go on. Victor says, 'I've always wanted to be free though I don't know what it means. You could pull out my nails and I still wouldn't be able to tell you. But it is all I want. First I was the prisoner of others and I dropped them, then of myself, so I dropped myself too. *Your* kind of liberty is false, ugly, used up, and you hang on to it so hard.'

Victor's way of escape is into total passivity. He considers that this is best for the time being, and death will be an even greater liberty. The Glazier thinks the discussion is now over: 'the

essential having been said', and the member of the audience
agrees they should not push things any further or they will end
up again in a fog. But, once more, any hopes that they have got
things sorted out are dashed, when Victor says: 'You know, what
I have just told you is not the truth. I only said it so you'd leave
me alone. I have something more to say'. The member of the
audience implores him not to say any more, it would spoil
everything. Victor requests 'two words', to which the member of
the audience magnanimously agrees. 'Two words, but no more.'
Victor says, 'I give up' (J'abandonne). The Glazier tells him not to
say that, now things are in order. Victor cries, 'I give up being
free'. 'This changes everything', says the man from the audience,
'what do you say?', he asks the Glazier, who replies, 'Je dis merde
[Pause] et remerde.'

The man from the audience thinks perhaps it is better this way,
and asks Victor: 'What will you do, what remains for you to do?'
Victor answers that he doesn't know, and the Glazier (shuddering)
cries: 'It's starting all over again. Say something, you *will* join the
boogie-woogie, yes or merde?'. This image of life as a dance
makes Victor smile. He says he will never be free but will continue
to seek freedom. Leaving 'joy' to others, he will content himself
with a calm state of limbo. Ordering everyone to get out he
returns to bed and turns his back on the audience. Curtain. In
this way he has the last word and ends the argument.

Eleuthéria provides a key to the later works. Echoing the themes
and humour of *Watt* and *Mercier and Camier*, with glimpses, in
Victor, of *Molloy*, it is, as Beckett said, 'part of the series'.
Described as 'a farce' and dealing with the serious theme of
freedom, it bears out what the representative of the audience said:
'It is what the best writers do. They give their most serious works
this description, in case they are not taken seriously.' This is the
key passage which prefigures Beckett's declaration in *Endgame*
that 'The most serious things are the funniest', an important step
towards the *risus purus*, the laugh which laughs at what is
unhappy.

6

The Trilogy: 'Prime, Death, Limbo'

The eponymous hero of *Molloy*, written in French, May–November 1947 (published 1951), is another divided character, a descendant of Murphy. Molloy has 'two, if not more, personalities' which he thinks is an advantage because he was 'never disappointed' whatever he did.

> in me there have always been two fools, among others, one asking nothing better than to stay where he is and the other imagining that life might be slightly less horrible a little further on, so that I was never disappointed, so to speak, whatever I did in this domain. And these inseparable fools I indulged turn about that they might understand their foolishness. (p. 51)

He derives from his multi-personality enough amusement to compensate for his own and the world's drawbacks. He knows there is a more joyous view of life than the one he has chosen, but it suits him to be gloomy. He says he 'takes care not to be gladdened by the sun . . . . The pale gloom of rainy days was better fitted to my taste.' When he says he is 'out of sorts' he means to be funny, and his definition of 'out of sorts' is the opposite of normal usage, for he points out: 'they are deep, my sorts, a deep ditch, and I am not often out of them, that's why I mention it' (p. 20). He was not born under a fortunate star. I am 'rather inclined to plunge headlong into the shit', he remarks ruefully (p. 33), but he contrives not to care; 'tears and laughter', he says, 'they are so much Gaelic to me'.

He is as phlegmatic about his physical disabilities as he is about his psychic difficulties; 'my two legs are as stiff as a life sentence' (p. 65), he tells us. But his mental impediments are worse, his reasoning is muddled, his ideas confused, his notions undirected: 'Oh they weren't notions like yours, they were notions like mine', he tells the reader, 'all spasm, sweat and trembling, without an

atom of common sense or lucidity. But they were the best I had'
(p. 72). His ideas about existence are different from those of
ordinary mortals, he would not go so far, he says, as to say he
saw 'the world upside down (that would have been too easy)',
but he saw it 'in a way inordinately formal, though I was far from
being an aesthete or an artist' (p. 53).

Beckett has said: 'I am not an intellectual, I am only a sensibility.
I conceived *Molloy* and what followed the day I became aware of
my stupidity. Then I began to write the things I feel'.[1] Although
he had already drawn on his own experience, as a student, in
More Pricks than Kicks, or as an exile in London, in *Murphy*, he had
not dug as deeply into his own unconscious as he was about to
do in the *Trilogy*. In *Molloy* the strain this exploration put upon
him was already beginning to show, for he was no longer
protected by the distance he put between himself and his heroes
in the earlier novels. He knew this, and in a letter to T. MacGreevy
he wrote: 'Molloy is a long book, the second last of the series
begun with Murphy, if it can be called a series. The last is begun
and then I hope I'll hear no more of him.'[2] Molloy himself
expressed much the same sentiment: 'This time, then once more I
think, then perhaps a last time, then I think it'll be over with this
world too' (p. 8). Like Beckett, Molloy is a writer, and, like
Beckett, he has reached the stage when he wants to say the last
things, 'say his goodbyes' (p. 7). Now that he feels he is within
sight of the end of his labours, the writer, Molloy, exploits his
own personality and experience in order to keep writing. To keep
writing is crucial, for the only certainty he has is that he must go
on writing (p. 13): 'Not to want to say, not to know what you
want to say, not to be able to say what you think you want to say
and never stop saying, or hardly ever, that is the thing to keep in
mind . . .' (p. 29). He does not write for money, nor does he
know why he writes, but thinks maybe it is to find the truth,
through telling things the way they are. This is beset with pitfalls,
the failings of the writer himself are not the least of them, he
thinks: 'Perhaps I'm inventing a little, perhaps embellishing, but
on the whole that's the way it was' (p. 8). The use of the word
'embellishing' is ironical, because nothing here is embellished.
The difficulties of telling the truth and the inexactness of
information are, however, often made comical, for instance, in
describing a dog: 'a pomeranian, I think, but I don't think so . . . .
Yes it was an orange pomeranian, the less I think of it the more

certain I am. And yet' (p. 12). The frustration caused by the
elusiveness of the truth is exacerbated by the impossibility of
saying anything in a new, more exact, way, as Molloy puts it:

> Saying is inventing, wrong, very rightly wrong. You invent
> nothing. You think you are inventing, you think you are
> escaping, and all you do is stammer out your lesson, the
> remnants of a pensum one day got by heart and long forgotten.
> (p. 33)

Though his inventions weary him, Molloy says that others still
beckon, in spite of his fatigue and his belief that 'you would do
better, at least no worse, to obliterate texts than to blacken
margins' (p. 13). He plunges into a seven-page digression on the
seaside, a benign experience, and a comic digression on his
system of sucking and pocketing stones in rotation. With only
two pockets this system resulted in uneven distribution though:
'It is true a kind of equilibrium was reached at a given moment, in
the early stages of each cycle, namely after the third suck and
before the fourth, but it did not last long' (p. 72). Finally he
reduces himself to one stone with the not surprising explanation
that 'they all tasted exactly the same'.

Such digressions are the chief source of humour in *Molloy* and
there is an important one on love which, in his much-quoted
opinion, is 'A mug's game . . . and tiring on top of that in the
long run' (p. 60). The first love affair he mentions, with a chamber
maid, is later denied: 'I should never have mentioned her . . .
perhaps there was no chambermaid'. This thought stirs him as a
writer, and he invents a title for this probably non-existent love
story: 'Molloy, or life without a chambermaid'. So we are warned
from the beginning that his ideas here about love are, as usual,
humorous. He has an affair with an elderly lady (Ruth, or Edith,
he cannot remember), whom he meets while he is probing a
rubbish dump, 'probably saying at that age, I must still have been
capable of general ideas. This is life' (p. 61). After each session
she gives him money, 'to me who would have consented to know
love, and probe it to its bottom, without charge'. But, he says,
'she was an idealist', or, funnier in French, 'elle n'était pas une
femme pratique'. He says this was his only experience of love,
and asks the reader to forget the chambermaid (p. 62). When he
runs over and kills Mrs Lousse's dog Teddy, she forces him to

take the dog's place in her affections, locking him in a room, at which he remarks to himself, 'If only your poor mother could see you now', then, criticising his own style: 'I am no enemy of the commonplace' (p. 41). Lousse attempts to 'soften him up' (as he mischievously phrases it) with food and drink, Circe-style drink ('miserable molys'). He says: 'doubtless she had poisoned my beer with something intended to mollify me', and, enjoying the pun, 'to mollify Molloy, with the result that I was nothing more than a lump of melting wax, so to speak' (p. 50); an image which originates in *More Pricks than Kicks*. He accepts the food and drink, despite the 'noxious and insipid powders and potions', but, he says, 'even sipid they would have made no difference, I would have swallowed it all down with the same wholeheartedness' (p. 56). In the end, though, he tires of 'love', and escapes to continue the quest.

This quest keeps Molloy eternally on the move, and he begins the journey on a bicycle (prime symbol of freedom in Beckett's works): 'Crippled though I was, I was no mean cyclist at that period. This is how I went about it. I fastened my crutches to the crossbar, one on either side. I propped the foot of my stiff leg (I forget which, now they're both stiff) on the projecting front axle, and I pedalled with the other' (p. 16). This bicycle is the source of Molloy's greatest pleasure: 'It was a chainless bicycle with a freewheel, if such a bicycle exists. Dear bicycle, I shall not call you bike ... .'. The bicycle has a horn, compounding Molloy's delight:

> To blow this horn was for me a real pleasure, almost a vice. I will go further and declare that if I were obliged to record, in a roll of honour, those activities which in the course of my interminable existence have given me only a mild pain in the balls, the blowing of a rubber horn – toot! – would figure among the first . . . . This should all be written in the pluperfect. (pp. 16–17)

Despite the drawbacks of being crippled, his fey outlook, and hang-ups about his mother, Molloy is one of Beckett's survivors. When he loses his bicycle he is philosophical:

> There is rapture, or there could be, in the motion crutches give. It is a series of little flights, skimming the ground. You take off, you land, through the thronging sound in wind and limb, who

have to fasten one foot to the ground before they dare lift up the other. And even their most joyous hastening is less aerial than my hobble. (p. 68)

For Molloy's consolations are in his head: 'I was no ordinary cripple, far from it, and there were days when my legs were the best part of me, with the exception of the brain capable of forming such a judgement' (p. 88). Even when reduced to crawling on his belly he finds compensations in his turn of thought: 'He who moves in this way, like a reptile, no sooner comes to rest than he begins to rest, and even the very movement is a kind of rest, compared to other movements . . .' (p. 96). Thus Molloy illustrates the art of survival, by adapting to change, and keeping on the move.

The importance of the quest in *Molloy* cannot be over-emphasised. For Molloy it is a way of life. Moran has his quest thrust upon him, he accepts it reluctantly, yet it has a great influence upon him as a character, as he becomes reflective and adaptable in adversity, less bourgeois and restricted in his views. In the opening stages of his journey, Moran is the type, *l'homme moyen sensuel*; there are many descriptions of his house, his garden, of his clothes, of his habits, of his food and drink. He tends to be vulgar and jolly, and so does his humour, which is often directed against the church or has sexual connotations.

On this level he can be quite funny. Irish stew, for instance: 'a nourishing and economical dish, if a little indigestible', excites the exclamation: 'All honour to the land it has brought before the world' (p. 105). Remarking that his son has a genius for geography, he adds lewdly: 'it was from him I learned that Condom is on the Baise'. He says the priest, by fasting, 'kills two birds with one stone', 'by way of mortification certainly, and then because his doctor advised it'.

Like Molloy, Moran is a writer, though not of literature: 'paltry scrivening' . . . 'is not part of my province' (p. 141), but of reports, for he is an agent, a private detective, and he receives a message from the Chief, Youdi, via his messenger Gaber, that he must retrieve, and write a report on Molloy, an assignment he accepts out of fear of Youdi, but unwillingly. Former clients whom Moran mentions by name are Yerk (this affair took three months we are told), Murphy, Watt and Mercier (p. 147), whom he describes as 'a rabble in my head, what a gallery of moribunds'

(p. 147). He says there were others. Molloy (maybe Mollose, he thinks) he knows, though he wonders if he invented him: 'There is no doubt one sometimes meets with strangers who are not entire strangers, through their having played a part in certain cerebral reels' (p. 120), an image of reels in the sense of film, or of dancing. Moran knew Molloy's mother, and is intimate with the Molloy family. Molloy himself, he sees as a prisoner, misshapen, hunted, uttering incomprehensible words, forever on the move, and he cannot understand why he, Moran, who is calm and reasonable, should be haunted by such a chimera (p. 122). Nevertheless he leaves his comfortable home, with his son, in search of Molloy. This quest proves onerous and destructive, but has its brighter moments, among them a bicycle, about which Moran exclaims: 'I would gladly describe it, I would gladly write four thousand words on it alone' (p. 166), as he experiences the same euphoria as Molloy did, when riding it.

Moran's quest is unsuccessful, he never finds Molloy, and finally, deserted by his son, with only his umbrella, bag, and fifteen shillings, and dreading Youdi's punishments, he sees the wretchedness of his situation and is seized with 'such a mighty fit of laughing' that he shook and, like Watt, has to 'lean against a tree, or against a bush' (p. 174). Laughing at his own misery, he feels transported beyond his own consciousness, though, as he humorously remarks, combining the poetic and the scatological, his self did not seem far from him at moments, when he 'seemed to be drawing towards it as the sands toward the wave, when it crests and whitens, though I must say this image hardly fitted my situation, which was rather that of the turd waiting for the flush' (p. 174). This laugh of Moran's can be recognised as the *risus purus*, the laugh at what is unhappy, 'the laugh of laughs'. Nothing, however terrible, can affect him now, for he has acquired the inner resources which distance him from his afflictions.

Molloy is a psychoanalytical riddle, a more sophisticated *Murphy*; the writer in quest of himself. Moran is the recorder, retriever of material; Molloy the creative side of the writer, whose consciousness provides Moran's sources. And we remember that Moran has worked to retrieve other characters of Beckett's, among them, Murphy, Watt, Mercier. Molloy and Moran, then, are two sides of one persona – a writer's – and as Moran says, when one dies the other will die too. Conversely, while one survives, so will the other, and the writing must continue, for, as Moran says, the quest was not for Molloy (who mattered nothing to him) nor for himself (of whom he despaired) but was more important than either of them. It was: 'on behalf of a cause which, while having need of us to be accomplished, was in its essence anonymous, and would subsist, haunting the minds of men, when its miserable artisans should be no more' (p. 123).

Written in 1948, in French, published 1951, *Malone Dies* is a sequel to *Molloy*, a further step in the quest for self of the writer Molloy/Moran, now called Malone: 'a kind of inventory' (p. 9). *Molloy* was originally to have been followed by one other book, *Malone Dies*: 'Cette fois-ci, puis encore une je pense, puis c'en sera fini je pense, de ce monde-là aussi.' When it was translated into English, *two* more books were envisaged, to make a trilogy: 'This time, then once more I think, then perhaps a last time, then I think it'll be over, with that world too' (p. 8). The third book was to be *The Unnamable*, and Beckett has said that the Trilogy can be seen as three phases of one existence: prime, death, limbo.[3] So, in *Malone Dies*, we have reached the second stage, death. Although the subject is not conducive to light comedy, a certain grim humour can be, and is here, wrung from it.

The stage he had reached in his exploration of man's vulnerability, ignorance, impotence, in this book which deals with death, seemed satisfactory to Beckett, who wrote to T. MacGreevy: 'I see a little clearly at last what my writing is about and I fear I have about perhaps ten years' courage and energy to get the job done. The feeling of getting oneself in perfection is a strange one, after so many years of expression in blindness.'[4] The same sentiment is expressed by the narrator in *Malone Dies*: 'Perhaps I have another ten years ahead of me', 'This time I know where I am going, it is no longer the ancient night, the recent night. Now it is a game I am going to play, I never knew how to play until now' (p. 8). The 'game' is to pass the time as he waits to die, and consists in telling himself stories, producing an inventory; 'making the tot' (p. 10) and perhaps writing his memoirs, though he calls the latter a joke (p. 12). Malone's memoir is not merely a joke, however, it is the continuing search for self, the recapitulation of his own story through the medium of the digressions on the youth, Sapo, and the young man, MacMann.

In *Malone Dies*, the narrator is satisfied that he has become a writer, and has achieved his own youthful aim. He now looks back through Sapo and MacMann, on the life he did not truly live because of his commitment to be a writer, (a theme which he develops later in *Krapp's Last Tape*): 'So I near the goal I set myself in my young days and which prevented me from living. And on the threshold of being no more I succeed in being another. Very pretty' (p. 22). He tells us his way was 'away from the living': 'The living. They were always more than I could bear . . . groaning with tedium I watched them come and go, I killed them, or took their place, or fled' (p. 22). '. . . I fled to my shadows as to sanctuary' (p. 23). Now, paradoxically, having never really lived he has retained access to his earlier innocence and can look back in comparative tranquillity, to relive the happy moments of youth, which was clouded at the time by his anxiety. He wants to relive that time before he dies: 'Between now and then I have time to frolic, ashore, in the brave company I have always longed for, always searched for' (p. 22). Characteristically, though, he fears this indulgence will destroy his hard won individualism and that, if he goes on living in the past, his present self will be lost: 'And I shall resemble the wretches famed in fable, crushed beneath the weight of their wish come true' (p. 22). Yet he feels compelled to recall his past, which has been impossible till now: 'Of myself I could never tell', he says, 'any more than live'. 'To show myself now, on the point of vanishing . . . that would be no ordinary last straw' (p. 24). He will accomplish this, he thinks, through telling himself stories.

To pass the time as he lies immobile, waiting to die, Malone says he will tell three stories: about 'an animal (a bird probably), a man and a woman, and a thing, probably a stone'. The story about the animal, probably a bird, is never told, though birds are touched on: there is a joke about vultures. Outside his window he sees all sorts of birds: 'They come and perch on the window-sill, asking for food! It is touching. They rap on the window-pane with their beaks. I never give them anything. But they still come, what are they waiting for?' Dying as he is, he is capable of a grim jest: 'They are not vultures' (p. 13).

There is an intellectual guffaw about a parrot which will only repeat the first three words of *Nihil in intellectu quod non prius in sensu* (There is nothing in the mind which is not first felt through the senses) (p. 46), thus: '*Nihil in intellectu . . .*', followed by squawks, close to Lucky's pseudo-intellectual speech in *Waiting for Godot*, which also is interrupted by squawks of 'qua qua qua'. Parrots, or parakeets, inspire a fantastic pun, confusing the

Paraclete (God the Holy Ghost, or Dove), and a parakeet. When Malone thinks he will never finish his inventory he remarks: 'a little bird tells me so, the paraclete, perhaps, psittacaceously named'. (Psittacaceously seems to be an invented word based on 'psittacosis' a disease of parrots) (p. 78).)

The story about the stone is even more tenuous, for he never gets to grips with it, but the story about the man and woman is illuminating, because this description covers Sapo's complacent parents and also the story about the deprived Lamberts, who are the objects of Sapo's youthful concern. The story of the Lamberts is described as 'mortal tedium', and is about the harsh life led by poor peasants. Lambert, the inarticulate pig-killer, only lively 'during the killing season', alarms his sick wife and children with blow-by-blow accounts of his pig-killing activities. Sapo compassionately observes their poverty and hard labour: 'so much work, so little time, so few hands' (p. 30), 'bent over the unyielding earth'. The story is not long, because the narrator cannot write about it without pain: 'No, I can't do it' (p. 24). Indignantly, yet with comic relief, he contrasts their lot with that of Sapo's fairly wealthy family.

Sapo is youthfully critical of his muddle-headed, narrow-minded, middle-class parents, scathingly recalling their 'axioms' and 'vague palavers' about money; he is not surprised they 'never led to anything'. One of their axioms is that a garden without roses, lawns and tidy paths is a 'criminal absurdity', a contrast with the Lamberts' dependence for a living on their piece of unproductive earth. Their ineffectual arguments about money, for instance Sapo's coaching fees, are recorded: 'You will have us in the poor house', says Mrs Sapo: 'It is an investment', says his father. Earnest and misguided, they blame such expenses for their inability to buy a load of manure to grow vegetables, and illogically look forward to old age, when they will retire to a cottage where, 'having no need of manure, they will be able to afford to buy it in cart-loads' (p. 16). This early joke seems to have gone deep with Beckett, and is revived in *All that Fall*, when the aged Maddy, offered such a load, asks what she would want with manure at her time of life.

Sapo perceives the Saposcats' want of understanding. They use their verbal exchanges as mere signals: 'Starting from a given theme their minds laboured in unison. They had no conversation properly speaking. They made use of the spoken word in much the same way as the guard of a train makes use of his flags or of his lantern' (p. 17). They want Sapo to be a doctor. 'He will look after us when we are old', says Mrs Sapo. 'What tedium', says the narrator, 'And I call that playing', and adds, 'I wonder if I am not talking yet again about myself'. He finds Mrs Sapo's ambition tedious, and also her attitude to religion: 'her piety grew warm at times of crisis', he tells us. He scathingly quotes her comic down-to-earth prayer for success in his examination: 'Oh God grant he pass, grant he pass, grant he scrape through' (p. 38).

The narrator finds it hard to discuss Sapo himself. He begins hopefully: 'Sapo loved nature', but cannot carry on. Sapo's dreams, doubts, desires, his longing for freedom are mentioned, but not developed. The narrator wonders at the patience and reason of this, his younger self, and marvels at how different Sapo was from himself, the narrator, at the present time. The thread of Sapo's story disappears, but is retrieved twenty pages later when he has become MacMann. In appearance he now resembles Watt, and the narrator wonders what has changed him so: 'Life perhaps, the struggle for love?'. He says, 'I slip into him, I suppose in the hope of learning something'. The narrator is more critical of MacMann than of Sapo, his younger self, reminding us of his attitude to Watt. MacMann is described as 'of the earth, earthy, and ill-fitted for pure reason', being 'no more than human, than the son and grandson and great-grandson of humans . . . it sometimes seemed that he would grovel and wallow in his mortality until the end of time and not have done' (pp. 69–70).

Like Belacqua, he is impossibly indolent: 'A good half of his existence must have been spent in a motionlessness akin to that of stone.' . . . 'It must be presumed', says the storyteller tartly, 'that he received from his numerous forbears, through the agency of his papa and mama, a cast-iron vegetative system, to have reached the age he has just reached, which is nothing or very little compared to the age he will reach, as I know to my cost, without any serious mishap' (p. 72). MacMann is confined in an institution reminiscent of that in *Watt*, and, as Watt meets and confides in Samuel, so MacMann meets and confides in Lemuel, in that institution.

It is here that the cruelly comic account of MacMann's love affair with Moll, his keeper, is situated. The development of this relationship is a source of bawdy humour, particularly their often-quoted ineffectual coupling: It was only natural, we are told, 'they should not succeed at first shot, given their age and experience', but, 'warming to their work' they eventually obtain 'a kind of sombre gratification', at which Moll exclaims 'being (at that stage) the more expansive of the two, Oh would we had met sixty years ago' (p. 89). The discrepancy between romantic aspirations and what they could achieve is pin-pointed in this encounter, ridiculed and made comic, but does result in MacMann's 'obtaining some insight into the meaning of the expression Two is company'. Moll's letters, too, are a target for irreverent wit, too funny to be merely cruel. We are told they did not vary much in form and tenor, and are given an example: 'Sweetheart . . . Ah would we had met seventy yers ago! No, all is for the best, we shall not have time to grow to loathe each other, to see our youth slip by, to recall with nausea that ancient rapture . . .' (p. 90), a satirical allusion to the perishability of human loves, and the universal frailty of mankind in this connection. Although Moll's letters are funny there is something touching and poetic about them: 'When you hold me in your arms, and I you in mine, it naturally does not amount to much, compared with the transports of youth, and even middle age . . . but it is the season of love, let us make the most of it, there are pears that only ripen in December' (p. 90). We are told that MacMann never answered her letters but, 'towards the close of this idyll, that is to say when it was too late, he began to compose brief rimes of curious structure, to offer his mistress'. There is a send up here ('rimes', 'mistress') of Elizabethan love poetry, in particular that of Donne, for the 'rimes' are 'remarkable for their exaltation of love regarded as a thing of lethal glue, a conception frequently to be met with in mystic texts' (p. 92), a momentary reprise of the youthful intellectual humour in the early novels.

The 'idyll' ends when Moll tires, though we are told: 'our concern here is not with Moll, who after all is only a female, but with MacMann, and not with the close of their relations, but rather with the beginning. Of the brief period of plenitude between these two extremes, when between the warming up of one party and the cooling down of the other there was established a fleeting equality of temperature, no further mention will be made' (p. 92). The account ends abruptly with the offer of 'a few more words in conclusion on the decline of this liaison', and the immediate refusal to give it: 'No, I can't' (p. 93). This is virtually the end of the story of Sapo/MacMann. The last we see of MacMann is when he is carried off with Murphy, Watt, Moran and other inmates of the institution by Lemuel, after the violence which ended the ill-fated boat trip to the island. However, at the time of MacMann's disappearance, the narrator reminds us he himself is still there: 'A few lines to remind me I too subsist . . . . My story ended I'll be living yet' (p. 113).

The story of Sapo/MacMann is not the only way the narrator traces his own life. The making of the inventory is another metaphor for the review of his development, 'making the tot'. This inventory covers a collection of bric à brac he has found, grown fond of and not discarded (he does discard some of the objects he finds). Among these possessions are smooth things he likes to finger, a stone, a horse-chestnut, a cone, also a broken pipe, a boot, a hat which reminds him of the good old days, though he says he remembers them well anyway, and a photograph of a donkey. But for the company of these objects, which gave him the impression they needed him, he confides engagingly: 'I might have been reduced to the society of nice people or the consolations of some religion or other, but I think not' (p. 77). However, he warns us not to over-estimate the significance of this inventory because, along with the stories of Sapo, Moll, his doubts and possessions, it is only a pretext to hold off death. Enlarging on this theme, in a drowning image he continues: 'pretext for not coming to the point, the abandoning, the raising of the arms and going down without a further splash', which finishes with a characteristically throw-away comic line, 'even though it may annoy the bathers' (p. 106). So, through the medium of his stories, memoir, and inventory, he has succeeded in holding off death, by continuing to speak.

As for writing, he says his quest as writer only began because his thoughts got lost, unless they were recorded, 'I did not want to write, but I had to resign myself to it in the end. It is in order to know where I have got to . . .' (p. 36). Writing has been difficult. At first the characters came to him 'pleased that someone wanted to play with them' (p. 46), but he failed to establish a relationship with them, he, Malone, he says, has never got on with people. 'Johnson, Wilson, Nicholson and Watson, all whoresons', disliked him. He has even tried the 'inferior races, red, yellow, chocolate', and would have tried the plague-stricken if he could have found any (p. 46). 'With the insane too I failed, by a hair's breadth' (p. 47). There is a reminder here of Murphy.

In the almost impossible task of expressing the inexpressible, Malone says, he has even tried 'shapelessness and speechlessness' (p. 46), probably a reference to *Watt*. Words have been his bugbear and they nearly got the better of him; for instance, the phrase 'Nothing is more real than nothing': 'They rise up out of the pit and know no rest until they drag you into its dark' (p. 21). But, he says, 'I am on my guard now'. He thinks the use of language is hazardous, but no worse than the things it tries to express: 'There is no use indicting words, they are no shoddier than what they peddle' (p. 23).

In such conditions, writing has been difficult, almost too difficult. He remedied this by beginning again, little by little with a different aim: 'no longer in order to succeed, but in order to fail. Nuance'. Traditional forms of writing were not capable of saying what he wanted to say about ignorance, or impotence, so he had to find a new way, less formal, to express the formless. Although, now, words and images run in his head, 'pursuing, flying, dashing, merging endlessly', he believes that 'beyond the tumult there is a great calm, and a great indifference, never really to be troubled by anything again' (p. 26).

He also believes that he will have to go on uttering to the end, and predicts that even after death he will not have finished testifying to the old story: 'My old story' (p. 64), which will be told without drawing any conclusions: 'without exaggeration, to be sure, quietly crying and laughing' (p. 8). And if he ever stops, he says, 'It will be because there is nothing more to be said, even though all has not been said, even though nothing has been said'. The thing is, he reminds himself, not to be discouraged: 'One of the thieves was saved, that is a generous percentage' (p. 83). The important thing is that the writing should go on, that whoever he is writing about should be given life: 'It is right that he should have his little chronicle, his memories, his reason, and be able to recognise the good in the bad, the bad in the worst, and so grow gently old all down the unchanging days and die one day like any other day, only shorter.'

The three phases of the narrator's existence, told in the Trilogy, prime (*Molloy*), death (*Malone Dies*), culminate in limbo: *The Unnamable*, finished in 1950 and published, in French, in 1952. *The*

Unnamable is consciously the end of an epoch: 'all this time I've journeyed, my adventures are over my say said' (p. 18). The tone is wry but not despairing. He writes from limbo where, blind and paralysed, he is 'stuck like a sheaf of flowers in a deep jar' (p. 43), and there is black irony in this comparison. He still has a written pensum to discharge before he can be free: 'as a punishment perhaps for having been born perhaps' (p. 26), and wonders how, in such conditions, he can write, 'to consider only the manual aspect of that bitter folly' (p. 17). His situation is desperate but he is still capable of humour. He starts his chronicle: 'The best would be not to begin. But I have to begin. That is to say I have to go on. I am obliged to speak. I shall never be silent. Never' (p. 8). He is not sure how to begin; whether his attitude should be sceptical ('*aporia* pure and simple' (p. 8)), or, by affirmations and negations, 'invalidated as uttered, or sooner or later' (p. 8). He decides on the latter, for he contradicts many of his statements. The one thing he is sure of is that the discourse must go on, so he invents 'obscurities, rhetoric' (p. 10). Paradoxically, it is his search 'to put an end to things, an end to speech', that keeps him writing (p. 16).

He says that now he will write, not of his masks, but of himself, 'that I see this, feel that, fear, hope, know and do not know' (p. 16). 'It's me now I must speak . . . it will be a step towards silence . . . . All these Murphys, Molloys and Malones do not fool me. They have made me waste my time, suffer for nothing, speak of them, when in order to stop speaking, I should have spoken of me and me alone . . . . Let them be gone . . . . There now there is no one here but me' (pp. 19–20). But what he is remains undecided, or what he hears or what he understands. What he knows is equally unsure, as he says in one of his arithmetical jokes: 'I manage to understand, oh not the half, nor the hundredth, nor the five thousandth, let us go on dividing by fifty, nor the quarter millionth, that's enough' (p. 105). Wearying of explanations, he hopes the preamble will soon come to an end, and a statement begin that will dispose of him (p. 18). It is now he who will take the stage, and not his masks, and he strides on, in a comic nautical image: 'Now it is I, I the creator, the beleaguerers have departed, I am master on board after the rats' (p. 110). The oration is based on Beckett's perennial preoccupation with God, mankind, time, diversions, particularly stories, words and silence. Keeping the nautical image, the Unnamable says he is on his way, 'words belly out my sails' (p. 69). But the moment of elation is brief. His thoughts on God, mankind, the diversions which help him along, are, he says, only ruses to keep writing, to keep going, and his sails are often slack.

In the Trilogy, Beckett has given up the pretence of an intellectual approach: 'the balls about being and existing . . . anything rather than these college quips' (p. 65), and is writing what he feels. He quips: 'I begin by the ear, that's the way to talk. Before that it was the night of time. Whereas ever since, what radiance!' But the senses can no more be trusted than can pure reason. The Unnamable describes the ear as 'Two holes and me in the middle, slightly choked' (p. 72). 'The eye, likewise.' He begins gaily: 'Ah yes there's great fun to be had from an eye, it weeps for the least thing, a yes, a no, the yesses make it weep, the noes too, the perhapses particularly' (p. 80), but, he concludes, jeering at the philosophical notion of *esse est percipi*: 'Balls all balls, I don't believe in the eye either, there's nothing here, nothing to see, nothing to see with, merciful coincidence when you think what it could be, a world without spectator, and vice versa, brr! No spectator then, and better still no spectacle, good riddance' (p. 92).

His view of mankind is no more optimistic. He thinks people are in a bad way, and says it is to be expected; they don't know who they are, nor where they are, nor what they're doing, not why everything is going so abominably badly: 'So they build up hypotheses that collapse on top of one another, it's human, a lobster couldn't do it. Ah a nice mess we're in, the whole pack of us' (p. 89). Man's fate is short and brutish, life a confidence trick enticing him: 'Come my lambkin, join our gambols, it's soon over, you'll see, just time to frolic with the lambkinette, that's jam – Love, there's a carrot never fails' (p. 32). Also, because of his nature, man asks too much and is disappointed: 'We must have the heavens and God knows what besides, lights, luminaries, the three-monthly ray of hope and gleam of consolation' (p. 71). He wearies of this theme, and brings it to an end: 'But let us close this parenthesis and, with a light heart, open the next' (p. 71). There is nothing more to be said on the subject, and he believes it is 'the everlasting third party' who is responsible for this state of affairs (p. 93).

Under the pseudonyms, 'third party' or 'the master', in scriptural phrases, the Unnamable lashes out at God, sometimes apologetically. He admits he has never paid much attention to him: 'No perhapses either, that old trick is worn to a thread. A few allusions here and there as to a satrap' (p. 28). He mentions 'Moran's boss, I forget his name' (he means Youdi), and thinks that maybe 'his will is done as far as I am concerned . . . and all is well with me without my knowing it' (p. 28), but complains, 'a little more explicitness on his part, since the initiative belongs to him, might be a help . . . In a word let him enlighten me, that's all I ask' (p. 29). It occurs to him that his master, perhaps, is not free to speak, and fantasises; perhaps he's part of a committee who cannot agree. Such a master, although he sympathises with him, he finds wanting. Though he feels in our dilemma we might end up needing him, he counsels against it, advising his readers to stick to their own kind, although they cannot expect to gain much from it: 'We have lost all sense of decency admittedly, but there are still certain depths we prefer not to sink to. Let's keep to the family circle, it's more intimate, we all know one another now, no surprises to be feared, the will has been opened, nothing for anybody' (p. 92).

When he momentarily runs out of topics, the Unnamable turns to diversions, as Vladimir and Estragon did, in order to keep going: 'I'm going to ask questions, that's a good stopgap', and he can't resist a pun, 'not that I'm in any danger of stopping'. He knows millions of questions, he says, and, when questions fail, there are always plans, he enthuses, and when plans fail there are aspirations: 'it's a knack, you must say it slowly. If only this, if only that, that gives you time, time for a cud of longing to rise up in the back of your gullet, nothing remains but to look as if you enjoyed chewing it, there's no knowing where it may lead you' (p. 119). He casts around for other stopgaps which prevent you from stopping: 'Hypotheses are like everything else, they help you on' (p. 122). What else, opinions comparisons . . . all helps, can't help helping, to get you over the pretty pass . . .', and he queries his own style and its fatuous expression: 'the things you have to listen to, what pretty pass?' (p. 119).

The Unnamable's chief diversion, like that of his predecessors, is telling stories. Although he has tried to give them up, he fears he will be obliged, in order not to peter out, to invent another fairy-tale: 'I hope and trust not. But I always can if necessary' (p. 23). He calls these stories facetiae, and says he would like to finish with his 'troop of lunatics', his 'ponderous chronicle of moribunds' (p. 24) who let him down, as media of expression.

Although he always hopes the next one will be better, he is doomed to disappointment. He makes a rueful joke of this: 'Unfortunately it is no help my being forewarned, I never remain so for long' (p. 63). But he has lost faith in stories, and says there's nothing to be got, there was never anything to be got from them (p. 93). There's no point, he says, in telling yourself stories to pass the time, they don't pass the time. The Unnamable says that when you have nothing left to say, you talk of time, seconds of time. There are some people, he says wistfully, who 'add them together to make a life. I can't'. All he knows about time is that it piles up about you deeper and deeper, 'your time, others' time, the time of the ancient dead and the dead yet unborn' (p. 107), and it buries you 'grain by grain', as Winnie is to prove, in *Happy Days*.

The Unnamable is disappointed, too, in his writing. Because of his obedience to the 'unintelligible terms of an incomprehensible damnation', he has written torrents of 'vain inventions', which have prevented him from uttering 'the true at last, the last at last'. He sees himself 'slipping, though not yet at the last extremity, towards the resort of the fable', and asks, would it not be better if he were simply to keep on saying babababa, for example, like a barbarian (p. 24). He does not think other writers have done any better, with 'their ballocks about life and death' (p. 102) and believes the only thing is to go on writing, without illusions about being able to conclude. But he does not despair, one day, he knows, he will go silent and make an end (p. 18). If what he writes is not clear he says, 'dear dear', he will go on seeking: 'I'm always seeking something, it's tiring in the end' (p. 104).

The fault is not so much in the writer, he thinks, as in the inadequacy of words, which are untrustworthy and carry meanings you do not intend: 'It seems impossible to speak and yet say nothing, you think you have succeeded, but you always overlook something, a little yes, a little no, enough to exterminate a regiment of dragoons' (p. 19). This battle image of words shows his recognition of his war with them. He complains that there is not much difference between one expression and another, and of the difficulties of interpretation. He says he understands the meaning of only one expression in a thousand, and extends this thought: 'Let us go on multiplying by ten, nothing more restful than arithmetic, in a hundred thousand, in a million.' He feels there is a mistake in this mathematical progression: 'it's too much, too little, we've gone wrong somewhere, no matter, there is no great difference between one expression and the next, when you've grasped one you've grasped them all, I am not in that fortunate position', and addresses himself: 'how you exaggerate, always out for the whole hog, the all of all, and the all of nothing . . . never in the happy golden' (p. 105–6). The Unnamable reiterates Beckett's contention that there is nothing new to say as well as no new way to say it; it is always the same old slush to be churned everlastingly, and quips, 'now it's slush, a minute ago it was dust, it must have rained' (p. 121).

Nevertheless he believes there's nothing else but words, 'you must go on, that's all I know . . . . You must say words as long as there are any, until they find me, until they say me . . . . Perhaps it's done already, perhaps they have said me already' (p. 132). Sometimes he is nothing but words himself, 'falling asunder' (p. 104), and he longs for the end of the 'wordy-gurdy' (p. 117). Luckily for him there are, from time to time, silences which he calls 'truces', in this battle with words, and the promise of silence, when 'all the words have been said, those it behoved to say' (he thinks they need not be more than a few) (p. 87). Here in the dark, he says, all he knows is that he needs words: 'I need them all, to be able to go on, it's a lie, a score would be plenty, tried and trusty, unforgettable, nicely varied, that would be palette enough, I'd mix them, I'd vary them, that would be gamut enough' (p. 126). He thinks that should keep him going until the end, which will be neither a bang nor a whimper; he thinks it may be a laugh, that's how it will end: 'in a chuckle, chuck, chuck, ow, bapa'. He says he will practise: 'yum, hoo, plop, pss', which, he says, represents nothing but emotion, 'bing bang, that's blows, ugh, pah'. What else? he enquires: 'ohh, aah, that's love, enough'. Then, (a joke of Malone's) 'It's tiring, hee hee' (p. 126).

This is a laugh in the tradition of the *risus purus*, the laugh which laughs at what is unhappy, but he still has to practise this laugh; he has not fully learned it, or completed his pensum to say it as it is. After a brief truce of silence he will have to continue the battle with writing: 'you must go on'. He thinks he cannot go on, but declares 'I'll go on'. The war with words is not yet over, and unlike Malone whose works gave him 'great satisfaction, some satisfaction', he is not satisfied.

Throughout the Trilogy, Beckett has chronicled the progress of a writer, and, in *The Unnamable*, he has attempted to sum it up.

But there are still too many undefined loose ends in this *pensum* to be able to recite the lesson of his learned experience. The struggle must continue, he thinks, in order to finish this part of his creative work and escape into silence, where life becomes a dream, though this too is doubtful. As the Unnamable says: 'All a dream, that would surprise me, a dream full of murmurs' (p. 132).

In *The Unnamable*, the narrator is turning to limbo, away from human existence, 'the wild dreams up above, under the skies' (p. 63), and towards silence, 'the dream silence full of murmurs'. Yet he is still preoccupied with the search for himself. He has said that the writing must go on till all the words have been said, 'until they have said me'. The stories of his masks, he says, are his story, part of his story, so it is necessary to repeat them in this light. Because he has not finished his quest for himself there are, after the Trilogy, continued reprises of themes and jests from the earlier works, notably in *Endgame* and *Krapp's Last Tape*. Like Hamm, he says 'no' to nothingness, and, like Krapp, he seeks relief in nature, in *jeux d'ésprit* and in nostalgia, but particularly in his compulsion to go on trying to tell it as it is.

7
Waiting for Godot

Waiting for Godot, written in 1949 and published in French in 1952 had the same function as *Eleuthéria* – to provide relief from the prose. It is significant that it was begun the year before the last part of the Trilogy, as Beckett said, to get away from the 'wildness and rulelessness of the novels'.[1] The play crystallises the view of existence which Beckett developed through the early works. The emphasis is on contradictions and uncertainties, the brevity of existence, the long wait for things to begin and for life to end, man's consternation in these conditions, offset by acid wit and his built-in determination to survive. *Waiting for Godot* echoes *Molloy* and *Malone Dies*, and looks forward to *The Unnamable*, so the four works give an impression of unity, with, in *Waiting for Godot*, the added dimension of knockabout comedy. The main theme which runs through *Waiting for Godot* – waiting – was already taking shape in *Malone Dies*: 'He who has been waiting long enough will wait forever. And there comes the hour when nothing more can happen and nobody more can come and all is ended but the waiting that knows itself in vain.' In a moment of discouragement Estragon echoes this: 'Nothing happens, nobody comes, nobody goes, it's awful' (p. 41). But he and Vladimir try to avoid being as negative as this.

More than any of Beckett's other works, *Waiting for Godot* illustrates the tensions between pathos and comedy, negation and affirmation, inertia and liveliness. The stage directions opening the first Act embody these contradictions: 'Estragon tries to take off his boot, tugging with both hands, panting with the effort. He gives up exhausted, and tries again. As before. The repetition of the action emphasises its importance.' Beckett has said that this is a mime of what the play is about: monotony.[2] Such unsuccessful action helps Vladimir and Estragon pass the time as they persist in waiting for something better, hoping the waiting is not in vain. Beckett subtitled *Waiting for Godot* 'A Tragicomedy' because his clown heroes will not accept their fate 'as true tragedy heroes would', here lies the comedy of the human condition.

94

Whereas in *Malone Dies* the general tone (apart from the may-hem at the end) is elegiac, almost tranquil – because Malone is trying to keep a balance between 'tears and laughter'; to be 'tepid', with-out enthusiasm – the tone of *Waiting for Godot* is sceptical, defiant, the humour ironical. The notions of resignation, *apatheia*, are firmly resisted, in this celebration of man's insistence on using his own will, however circumscribed, and determination to persist in his efforts. When Vladimir asks the blind Pozzo what he does, when he falls far from help, the answer is: 'We wait till we can get up. Then we go on.' Here the waiting and the determination to go on are combined. *Waiting for Godot* catalogues the ploys men use to combat discouragement and doubts, which make them comic and heroic.

The heroes of *Waiting for Godot*, Vladimir and Estragon, are down on their luck, but have seen better days. *The Unnamable* refers to them as a 'pseudo-couple', and it is possible that, like Mercier and Camier, they represent two sides of a single consciousness. They are complementary: one responsive, the other aggressive; one selfless, the other self-absorbed. They relate to each other, yet long to be free; understand each other, yet are opposed. From their wranglings and changes of mood comes the ambivalent comedy, which is also present in *Mercier and Camier*. Indeed there are overt reminders of the comic exchanges in *Mercier and Camier*. For example, the romantic Vladimir remembers landscapes, scenery. The sceptical Estragon scoffs: 'You and your landscapes. Tell me about the worms' (p. 61). Mercier and Camier also differed about the relative importance of the beauty of the bog, and the worms which inhabit it, and this is a metaphor for their opposing perceptions of life itself. Like Mercier and Camier, Vladimir and Estragon share a need for diversions in the longueurs of existence, and, as representatives of all mankind, a need for company, the prospect of which can always save Vladimir from the horrors: 'We are no longer alone, waiting for night, waiting for Godot, waiting for . . . waiting. All evening we have struggled unassisted. Now it's over. It's already tomorrow. Time flows again already. The sun will set, the moon will rise' (p. 77). As Vladimir says, we wait, we are bored to death (a play on the cliché, 'bored to death' and the literal, bored lifelong, until we die). Any diversions which come along, he said, should be used (p. 81). Their diversions are varied, and not always successful, but that does not deter Vladimir and Estragon, except momentarily, from thinking up new ones.

An important diversion of Vladimir's is religion, which he often ponders on. He is particularly concerned with the notion of guilt, human guilt. He thinks repentance might be the answer, but cannot think what humans should repent except, wryly, of being born; sending up the idea of original sin. Such questioning of religious dogma is a reminder of the intellectual humour of the early novels, and their criticism of Providence itself. When Vladimir speaks to the sceptical Estragon of the comforts of religion, and mentions 'our Saviour', Estragon, who does not feel saved, rudely asks 'Our what?' and enquires, 'Saved from what?'. When Vladimir answers 'Hell', Estragon is annoyed, because he feels he is in hell anyway. Vladimir is more hopeful than Estragon, and thinks, always, that tomorrow will be better (p. 52). He is constantly on the lookout for things to feed hope, though he is divided about it, because continuing to hope makes him feel both relieved and appalled (p. 52).

This uncertainty about hope is what *Waiting for Godot* is about, and the symbol of hope in this play is the seemingly dead tree, which produces leaves in the second Act. This event is tied to the two key motifs of the play, '. . . do not despair, one of the thieves was saved', which Vladimir, like Malone, describes as a reasonable percentage, and the Biblical proverb, which he quotes but cannot complete: 'Hope deferred maketh the heart sick, but when the desire cometh it is a tree of life' (Proverbs 13:12). Vladimir says about the bare scenery: 'It's indescribable. It's like nothing. There's nothing.' Then he adds a metaphor of life and hope: 'There's a tree'. From the beginning, the tree is the centre of their existence as well as of the stage; they meet by it, watch it, hide behind it. In moments of terror, they can even be funny about it. They decide it is a willow, they think it must be dead, and joke: 'no more weeping!'. Vladimir continues to hope it will burgeon: 'Perhaps it's not the season for leaves' (p. 13). Such intellectual jokes play an important part in this play in which various philosophies are mocked.

Vladimir and Estragon debate the whim of Providence, which makes you a Pozzo or a Lucky (p. 31), or whether they are tied to Godot (p. 19). They try out a stoical attitude, which does not last, that is, 'doing nothing, expecting nothing, accepting there's nothing to be done on this bitch of an earth': 'One can bide one's time. One knows what to expect. No further need to worry. Simply wait. We're used to it' (p. 38). This bores them and they look for new ploys. There is a play on Berkeley's notion of *esse est percipi*, when Vladimir asks the messenger to tell Godot he has seen them [Pause], 'You did see us, didn't you?'. In their game of imitating the willow, Estragon 'does the tree', and asks, turning this idea round: 'Do you think God sees me?'. In a parody of Coué's method of mind over matter, Vladimir tells Estragon: 'Say you are happy even if it's not true', and Estragon answers, 'What am I to say?'.

> V. Say I am happy.
> E. I am happy.
> V. So am I.
> E. So am I.
> V. We are happy.
> E. We are happy. (Silence) (p. 60)

Then he enquires: 'What do we do now, now that we are happy?'. But these philosophical jugglings have a purpose, as Estragon says, echoing Descartes' *cogito ergo sum*, 'We always find something, eh Didi, to give us the impression we exist?' (p. 69). Such pastimes not only pass the time, they also give a sense of identity. When they are stumped for new diversions, Estragon suggests they should turn resolutely towards Nature. 'We've tried that', says Vladimir. 'True', says Estragon, and this ends the debate, which Estragon describes as 'not such a bad little canter'. Vladimir says they will have to find something else to do. This results in a music-hall routine with hats (p. 65): 'Estragon. Let me see (he takes off his hat, concentrates). Vladimir. Let me see (he takes off his hat, concentrates). Long silence. Ah! (They put on their hats and relax).'

Such vaudeville acts provide the framework for the humour of *Waiting for Godot*. In a play on man's fall from grace, when he 'lost his rights', Vladimir and Estragon give a comic display of downheartedness, arms dangling, heads sunk, sagging at the knees (p. 19). Momentarily angry with Estragon's Job-like misery, Vladimir, halting violently, says: 'Will you stop whining. I've had my bellyful of your lamentations', but is cheered immediately when he finds Lucky's hat, and they go into another hat routine. There is a long stage direction on how to revolve three hats between them, and extra funny business when Vladimir minces about the stage like a mannequin, until they tire of the game. At the end of the play, after they decide to hang themselves tomorrow, there is the light relief of a Laurel and Hardy trouser-dropping scene (p. 94). This is a vital moment in the play about which Beckett wrote to Roger Blin that the audience's laughter at the trouser-dropping, which some critics thought out of character, was in the traditions of the preceding scenes: 'The spirit of the play, so far as it has one, is that nothing is more grotesque than the tragic', a thought which is repeated later, in *Endgame*.[3] Such a moment of farce defuses the terrors of existence, and is a vital weapon in Beckett's armoury against despair. It also emphasises the recognition, present in the early works, that life is a stage, the people merely players, an important step on the road to the *risus purus*, the laugh that 'laughs at the laugh', or at what is unhappy.

When the hermetic world of Molloy and Malone is transferred, in *Waiting for Godot*, to the stage, the joke is that the audience as well as the characters find themselves to be trapped: 'Let's go. We can't. Why not? We're waiting for Godot. (Despairingly) Ah!' Life is theatre, and the notion, developed in *The Unnamable*, is that we have paid our money so we have to watch the show. ('It's a public show. You buy your seat and you wait, perhaps it's free, a free show, you take your seat and you wait for it to begin, or perhaps it's compulsory, a compulsory show, you wait for the compulsory show to begin, it takes time . . . you hear a voice, . . . that's the show, you can't leave, you're afraid to leave, it might be worse elsewhere, you make the best of it' (*The Unnamable*, p. 99).) *Waiting for Godot* has become a universal metaphor for existential tedium, or worse, that cannot be escaped, and comic mileage is got from criticisms, not only of existence, but of the play itself, for instance when Vladimir and Estragon break off at a hiatus in the development of the Lucky/Pozzo theme, to criticise the inconsequentiality and vulgarity of the action, which is a metaphor for life:

> Charming evening we're having.
> Unforgettable.
> And it's not over.
> Apparently not.
> It's only the beginning.
> It's awful.
> Worse than the pantomime.
> The circus.

The music-hall.
The circus. (p. 35)

Thus, into the longueurs of *Waiting for Godot* is inserted a
succession of comic set pieces which help not only Vladimir and
Estragon, but the audience too, to continue with the play.

Often these comic interludes are based on exaggerations of
normal human behaviour. When Vladimir and Estragon are bored
with each other, for instance, they think they should part, but
remember that the alternative is worse: 'the beauty of the way,
the goodness of the wayfarers', as Estragon ironically describes it,
is too awful. So they decide to hang themselves instead. Comedy
is drawn from the difficulties of hanging oneself. The tensions
between the life-urge and death result in the bawdy thought that
hanging would result in an erection, which momentarily cheers
the would-be suicides. Then there is the comic argument whether
Vladimir should go first because he is heavier (he is not), as
Estragon, says: 'Gogo light – bough not break – Gogo dead. Didi
heavy – bough break – Didi alone' (p. 17). As a final explosion in
this display of pyrotechnics they decide not to do anything – it's
safer – and wait to consult Godot. This plan, again, is foiled by
uncertainty about Godot's reactions to their 'kind of prayer, vague
supplication'. Discussing this they use staccato vaudeville patter
which, as Beckett has said (*Proust*, p. 92), 'inaugurates the comedy
of exhaustive enumeration':

> And what did he reply?
> That he'd see.
> That he couldn't promise anything.
> That he'd have to think it over.
> In the quiet of his home.
> Consult his family.
> His friends.
> His agents.
> His correspondents.
> His books.
> His bank account.
> Before taking a decision,
> It's the normal thing.
> Is it not?

> I think it is.
> I think so too.
> *Silence.* (*Waiting for Godot*, p. 18)

Theatrical comic business sometimes draws in the audience, whose presence, as such, Vladimir and Estragon ignore. Facing the auditorium they speak of it as variously 'a charming spot, inspiring prospects' (p. 13), 'that bog' (p. 34), or a way of escape: 'There! Not a soul in sight. Off you go' (p. 74). In sending up the play, Vladimir and Estragon often criticise the dialogue. In one dull passage Estragon exclaims ironically: 'I find this most extraordinarily interesting' (p. 12). About a wrangle over a carrot, Vladimir says: 'This is becoming really insignificant', and Estragon replies: 'Not enough' (p. 68). Many comic effects rise from the variety of the dialogue. The language is generally simple, demotic; banalities and clichés abound, with highflown passages for comic contrast. Conversational exchanges, often *non sequiturs*, are meant only to keep the ball rolling; it is all a game, Vladimir tells Estragon: 'Come on Gogo, return the ball, can't you, once in a way' (p. 12). Estragon describes their talks as 'blathering about nothing in particular' (p. 65). But they are ingenious in finding topics. One session they begin formally, after trying to speak at once, a reprise of Mercier's and Camier's polite exchanges (p. 99):

> Oh, pardon!
> Carry on.
> No no, after you.
> No no, you first.
> I interrupted you.
> On the contrary.

Their politeness angers them and they become abusive:

> Morpion.
> Sewer rat.
> Curate.
> Cretin.
> (with finality) Crritic!

This is too much for Vladimir, he wilts, vanquished, and turns away. A reconciliation scene follows:

Now let's make it up
Gogo!
Didi!
Your hand!
Take it!
Come to my arms!
Your arms?
My breast!
Off we go!

They embrace. They separate. Silence (p. 75)

At the end of this absurd exchange Vladimir exclaims: 'How time flies when one has fun! (p. 76) and, again, the dramatic action parodies and illustrates the comic absurdity of human interaction.

The main burden of *Waiting for Godot* is that life is a joke on humankind, which, as far as it can, must make its own decisions. As Vladimir says: 'all mankind is us, whether we like it or not. Let us make the most of it, before it is too late. Let us represent worthily for once the foul brood to which a cruel fate consigned us!' (p. 79). He points out that there are more ways than one of doing this. We can be active, or passive: 'It is true that when with folded arms we weigh the pros and cons we are no less a credit to our species' (p. 80). Heavily ironical, Vladimir says that we know why we're here, to wait for Godot or for night to fall, as billions of others before us have done, with as little certainty and the same dusty answers. It seems that he agrees with Lucky that 'though God dearly loves us (with some exceptions) life is an abode of stones, in spite of the tennis' (p. 45). In other words, the humorous approach is the best riposte, and the ability to laugh at what is unhappy the best defence. Thus *Waiting for Godot* provided a respite in Beckett's effort to say what he had to say, tell it as it is, and his disappointment that he had not yet done this, and is an important step towards the *risus purus*.

8

'Impasse'

The Unnamable had failed for Beckett as the long-desired summing up, but it paved the way for a treasure house of echoes from the early works, and is a further stage in his artistic development. *Texts for Nothing*, finished in 1952 was published in French in 1954, in thirteen sporadic episodes dictated by a disembodied voice from limbo and described by him as 'fitfully received', 'The merest scraps', he says, 'are coming through'. He picks up the theme where *The Unnamable* left off and begins: 'Suddenly, no, at last, long last, I couldn't any more, I couldn't go on.' This marks the well-known 'impasse' which occurred in the early 1950s and which produced several abandoned works.

The wrestle, in *The Unnamable*, to say it as it is had temporarily alienated Beckett, even from his own unstable world, and in *Texts for Nothing*, his character, in Pirandellian fashion, lies in limbo waiting to be born, to be written. The author has invested this particular character with his own persona, and the character complains: 'he will not dignify me with the third person, like his other figments, not he, he'll be satisfied with nothing less for me, for his me.' 'When he had me, when he was me, he couldn't get rid of me quick enough' (p. 23). 'The truth is', says the character, 'he is looking for me to kill me, to have me dead like him' (p. 22). The character is, in fact, waiting for 'committal to the flesh as the dead are committed to the ground' (p. 51). Meanwhile he soliloquises, not unsympathetically, on the shortcomings of his author – 'here I'm a mere ventriloquist's dummy' (p. 42) – and confirms his sense of a possible existence by looking back on the past, which he shares with his author. 'That's how I've held on till now', he confides (p. 11).

All he is sure of is that not everything has been said, in the 'farrago of silence and words, . . . this pell mell babel silence and words' (p. 34). He is cautious, summing up cannot be hurried: 'One must not hasten to conclude, the risk of error is too great' (p. 39). So he will make a fresh start, and quips there is 'nothing like breathing your last to put new life in you' (p. 10), although 'one begins to be very tired, very tired of one's toil, very tired of one's quill' (p. 30).

There are still hopes, 'high hopes', that one day a story will be written: 'a little story with living creatures coming and going on a habitable earth' (p. 35), though there will be corpses in it, of course. He is indecisive about what kind of story, though it will be based on the author's life – 'what a life' – 'a mine' of material (p. 23). The comparative merits of the tragic and comic methods are discussed: 'Tears, that could be the tone, if they weren't so easy, the time, tone and tenor at last' (p. 35). But he cannot weep, he says, so comedy, is more suitable. A laugh distances the horrors, especially of oneself, he says (p. 28), and everything becomes a game (p. 29). It seems he will plump for something more difficult, neither comedy nor tragedy. But the writing must continue, he has to make sure he has 'left no stone unturned', he says, before 'reporting myself missing' and giving up (p. 36).

To produce a story, he feels he must escape from his twilight world, to the world above in the light: 'a week in spring, that puts the jizz in you' (p. 16). His way of escape is memory, and nostalgically he recalls the friendships and wandering years of former existence, and happier days, 'when I played all regardless or nearly, worked and played' (p. 34). Among the ghosts he arouses are Murphy (p. 18), Mercier and Camier and the other cronies, Vladimir and Estragon (p. 18), Molloy and Malone – who, though 'mere mortals', were happy, he says – (p. 23), Pozzo (p. 27) and himself as Watt (p. 37). About Watt he speculates: 'What if after all this time I had not stirred hand or foot from the third-class waiting room of the South Eastern Railway terminus . . . with its pretty neo-Doric colonnade . . . . Waiting for the dawn and the joy of being able to say I've the whole day before me, to go wrong, to go right, to calm down, to give up, I've nothing to fear, my ticket is valid for life' (p. 38). He has come on a bit since then, he implies, but is not sure it is in the right direction. 'So home to roost it comes', he says ironically, the 'old past ever new, ever ended, ever ending, with all its hidden treasures of promise for tomorrow, and of consolation for today' (p. 50). He thinks that this way he may find himself again, as he once was, though he cautiously reminds himself not to be too affirmative at this stage: 'it would not be in my interest' (p. 51).

However, his memories of these earlier characters reinforce him, he thinks he had something once and exults: 'This is most reassuring, after such a fright, and emboldens me to go on, once again' (p. 50). It is through such friendships, or relationships, that life has meaning. He thinks he will take the road again 'that cast me up here', and retraces the past, and (shades of Mercier and Camier, Vladimir and Estragon), he will have a crony: 'my own vintage, my own bog, a fellow warrior' (p. 18). The recapitulation of this friendship makes his language rather racy: 'We have not long, that's the spirit, in the present, not long to live, . . . halleluiah. We wonder what will carry us off in the end. He's gone in the wind, I in the prostate rather' (p. 18). 'We spend our life, it's ours, trying to bring together in the same instant a ray of sunshine and a free bench, in some oasis of public verdure, we've been seized by a love of nature, in our sere and yellow, it belongs to one and all, in places' (p. 19). Sitting in the park, a place where nature 'belongs to one and all', they devour the papers, beginning with the racing pages: 'The sport of kings is our passion' (p. 19). The friend, Vincent, spends his time, like Vladimir, in trying to nourish him. When he seemed to be failing, Vincent would 'ram the ghost back down my gullet with black pudding' (p. 19). He also nourished him spiritually: 'With his consolations, allusions to cancer, recollections of imperishable raptures, he'd prevent discouragement from sapping my foundations. And I, instead of concentrating on my own horizons, which might have enabled me to throw them under a lorry, would let my mind be taken off them by his' (p. 19). But, he says: 'that's old memories, last shifts older than the flood' (p. 20). Yet, through his recall of such characters, he feels he may know again what he once was and roughly who, 'and how to go on, and speak unaided, nicely, about number one and his pale imitations' (p. 51).

Because, opines the character, the fault lies with the author, who despised characters like Molloy and Malone, because they were 'merely mortal'. In reality, he says, he despised them for being ordinary, happy mortals (p. 23). The author, he thinks, would not like his story to be told like theirs, like 'a vulgar Molloy, a common Malone' (p. 23). 'Yes', says this latest, most elusive character, 'he'll be satisfied with nothing less than me, for his me' (p. 23). He thinks the author should not differentiate between his personae, because 'it's all the same dream, the same silence, it and me, it and him, him and me and all our train' (p. 63). He also thinks the author deceives himself as well as everyone else: 'Although he says he has no story he tells his story every five minutes, saying it's not his story, there's cleverness for you' (p. 23). And although he said he does not reason, he reasons all the time: 'crooked, as if that could improve matters' (p. 22). The character thinks the author would do better to give up, 'Forget me, know me not, yes, that would be the wisest' (p. 22), yet he sees he must go on.

The author's great problem, according to his character, is to resolve the tension between negation and affirmation: 'the yesses and noes mean nothing in this mouth' (p. 45). The author, he says, cannot even be negative up to the hilt, and, expressing the conflict in a violent image, his character enquires rhetorically: 'whose the screaming silence of no's knife in yes's wound?' (p. 63). 'Ah', he sighs: 'if no were content to cut yes's throat and never cut his own' (p. 42). He thinks what the author needs to bring his fruitless quest to an end in a new no to cancel 'all the old noes that buried me down here' (p. 56). Because the old noes are too insubstantial, 'dangling in the dark and swaying like a ladder of smoke, yes a new no that none says twice' (p. 57). It seems to his character unlikely that the author will ever find this definitive 'no'. It probably does not exist any more than a definitive 'yes', and, in perpetual uncertainty, he must, and will, continue to wrestle with the tragi-comic paradoxes of life's variety and at the same time its monotony, its agitation and at the same time calm, its 'vicissitudes within what changelessness' (p. 46).

The unachieved character sympathises with the author's endeavour. He knows that he 'wants to leave a trace, yes, like air leaves among the leaves' (p. 61), to make some statement, however tenuous, and he feels pity for the voice which has failed to give him existence, and which itself is dying away. Paradoxically, the pity he feels for the author gives the character the impression that perhaps he himself does exist, there is 'the faint hope of a faint being after all, human in kind' (p. 62). He feels he has 'a kind of conscience, and on top of that a kind of sensibility' (p. 27), and though 'there was never much talk of a heart, literal or figurative' there may be one some day, 'to send up to break in the galanty show' (p. 62). In a rare moment free of his customary introspection, the character thinks he is not alone in this long process of development: 'perhaps beside me, and all around, other souls are being licked into shape' (p. 51). And there is a hint that his relationship to his unsatisfactory author has a parallel in man's relationship to God. For he thinks there is 'reasoning' going on, which has a natural rhythm like the contrasts of 'the great colds, the great heats, the long days, the long nights' (p. 45). And, if there is eventually silence, it will not be yet, though the voice continues to murmur that all will be ended, all said (p. 63). In fact, as in *Waiting for Godot*, something is taking its course.

The humour of *Texts for Nothing* is more than customarily subtle, though there is the usual wit and wordplay. The unachieved character, waiting to be written, observes, echoing a joke from *First Love*, that in purgatory you may even believe yourself dead on condition you make no bones about it (p. 24). Or, absent for awhile, he heralds his return with a mathematical joke: 'Peekaboo, here I come again, just when most needed, like the square root of minus one' (p. 54). Disparaging the craft of writing, he uses a food image when he thinks he may utter 'another guzzle of words, but piping hot' (p. 52). Though he despises them, words are his lifeline and must be held on to: 'To need to groan and not be able, Jesus, better ration yourself' (p. 13). Frustrated by words, he howls 'that's right, wordshit, bury me avalanche and let there be no more talk' (p. 46).

The main humorous aspect of this work is that it is an apologia, presented by an unachieved character for his author: the 'weak old voice that tried in vain to make me' (p. 61). *Texts for Nothing* not only turns upside down traditional forms of writing, and sends up the notion of an omniscient author; it tackles the paradoxical nature of an existence full of contradictions, where 'no's knife is always turning in yes's wound', and illustrates the impossibility of being able to tell it as it is, yet at the same time declares a positive determination to do so.

After *Texts for Nothing*, Beckett's writing went through a difficult phase. He wrote in 1953 to Tom MacGreevy: 'I can't go on and I can't get back', adding hopefully, 'perhaps a play one day'. But first, he began and abandoned a novel, an early draft of which he marked: 'This text was written 1954 or 55. It was the first text written directly in English since *Watt* (1945).'[1] A fragment, 'From an Abandoned Work', appeared in *Trinity News*, a Dublin University weekly (7 June 1956) and was broadcast by the BBC in 1957. Its apologetically comic tone is reminiscent of *First Love*, its elegiac quality looks forward to *Endgame* and *Krapp's Last Tape*. The oblique language heralds that of the later reductionist works after *How It Is*.

The mood of 'From an Abandoned Work' is patient, almost resigned. The narrator looks forward to the time when, his pensum done, he has his reward, and all will be still: 'the old half-knowledge of when and where gone, and of what'. He says all was illusory – 'there was never anything, never can be, life or death, all nothing, that kind of thing'. All will be reduced, he says, to 'a voice dreaming and droning on all around, that is something, the voice that once was in your mouth' (p. 20).

This piece is important because it marks the transition, begun in *The Unnamable*, from the high-spirited early works. In it, Beckett is finding the long-sought method of expressing formlessness, which he developed in the later works. He is bidding goodbye to the comedy, desperate or good humoured of the early works, and looking forward to the time when laughter and tears conflict no more, though the wrestle with words must go on.

Between 1952 and 1955, Beckett also began and abandoned several other works,[2] among them three plays of significance in the development of the canon: 'Mime du Rêveur', an abandoned play in French, about characters called Ernest and Alice (1954 or 1955), and another unfinished play, 'The Gloaming' (1956). The 'Mime du Rêveur' is a mime for a single character in a rocking chair and looks forward to *Endgame* and *Krapp's Last Tape*. Its technique heralds the later *Breath* or *Film*.

The importance of the abandoned play, written in French, between 1952 and 1955, untitled and unpublished, lies in its significance as a run-up to *Endgame*. It is for two characters, Ernest and Alice, husband and wife, master and servant, and its sombre theme, like that of *Endgame*, is heightened by some wry humour. Ernest, like Hamm, is immobile while Alice, like Clov, ministers to his needs. Ernest's situation, however, is more bizarre than Hamm's, for he is crucified upside down. His situation brings forth some blasphemous quips. There are also echoes of earlier intellectual jokes about Beckett's other bugbear, bourgeois existence, its obsessions and hypocrisies.

The outrageous comedy in this abandoned play on the theme of religion is in the tradition of Beckett's bitter sending-up of religious themes, from *More Pricks than Kicks* onwards, as is his criticism of bourgeois values, which reached its height in *Eleuthéria*, another play which parodied 'real' life, particularly the tyrannies and hypocrisies of the Krapp family. Ernest's self-absorption has affinities with that of Belacqua or Murphy, and the 'seedy solipsists' of the Trilogy, but he has gone a stage further. This slight character sketch is developed and carried to its extreme in the later reductionist works in which Beckett's protagonists are totally withdrawn from the world of 'reality'. But in the meantime Ernest is to have another incarnation as Hamm, in *Endgame*, who hasn't yet finished with this world, or the contradictions of existence in it.

'The Gloaming', written in English in 1956, was published in French in 1974. This fragment of a play, in the form of a dialogue for a cripple and a blind man, takes a black view of the human condition; the vanity of human wishes on one hand, and the persistence of human nature in its shifts to survive, on the other. Once more, the characters in this play, A, the blind man, and B, the cripple, have different viewpoints, aims and needs. But ultimately, in the fight for existence, they need each other's help. The cripple suggests they set up house together as they are 'made for each other', a typically Beckettian black comic notion. Like Watt and Mrs Gorman it is their disabilities, not their finer points, which are complementary and which make them attractive one to the other. In their conflicts and dependence upon each other, A and B look back to all the couples, or 'pseudo-couples', from Mercier and Camier, and forward to Hamm and Clov, the last of their line. Mordant humour is extracted from the tension between B's need for love, which would 'reconcile' him to his fellow beings (p. 69) and A's disgust with the human race. The themes of loss and adaptation to it are, as always, a source of black humour. A says that before his lost violin he had a harp, which he also lost. B jests that, now he has lost the violin, he will tell someone else one day that, before he had a harmonica, he had a violin, and taunts A: when he has lost the harmonica he may be reduced to having to sing.

Although these pieces are mere fragments, they echo the slapstick and tragicomedy of the earlier works, particularly the Trilogy, and, more important, prepare the way for *Endgame* and *Krapp's Last Tape* in which, the narrator having broken through the writing block, or impasse, is consciously making 'the tot' of all that has gone before.

9

'The laugh of laughs laughing at what is unhappy'

Written in French in 1956 and published in 1957, *Endgame* was described by Beckett as rather difficult and elliptic. Yet concealed in its obscurities is one of the clearest of all the statements he has made about the antinomies of the human condition; on the one hand the seeming absurdity of existence, and on the other the perception of a continuing chain of being. He reaches no conclusion but there is a sense of 'something taking its course'.

Beckett has said that in this play there are no accidents, everything is based on analogy and repetition. The action of the play has an affinity with the repetitive, defensive play at the end of a less-than-perfect chess game which is a metaphor for life. In this particular endgame, Hamm is immovable at the centre of the stage. Clov moves, against his will, but prefers a remote position in his kitchen. The pawns make only the feeblest moves, until Hamm orders them to be 'bottled' and the lids are put on. Beckett has said: 'Hamm is a king in this chess game, lost from the start. From the start he knows he is making loud senseless moves. That he will make no progress at all . . . . Now at last he makes a few senseless moves as only a bad player would. A good one would have given up long ago. He is only trying to delay the inevitable end. Each of his gestures is one of the last useless moves which put off the end.'[1]

This game is like the 'dud chess game' in *Eleuthéria*, in which the onlookers long to intervene so they can go home to bed. Or, again, the long defensive game played by Mr Endon with Murphy, which gets them nowhere. The main function of each of these games is to pass the time during the long wait for extinction, a situation which is not without humour *chez* Beckett, and not without its positive aspects. This play, like *Mercier and Camier*, or *Waiting for Godot* presents opposing points of view about human existence, and there is a feeling that despite the evidence to the contrary, there is some meaning behind it. The play is not to win – which is impossible – but to delay the end with a dialogue on existence, perhaps from the points of view of one divided person, as in *Mercier and Camier*, or *Waiting for Godot*, with the usual Beckettian banter, fantasy, nostalgia, old jokes, comic exchanges and black humour. *Endgame*, like *Waiting for Godot*, is a tragicomedy; pathos and bathos are interrelated as they are in life.

The likeness to *Waiting for Godot* is not fortuitous. Beckett told Roger Blin that Hamm and Clov are Didi and Gogo at a later date, 'at the end of their lives',[2] and indeed both pairs of characters are opposites: Clov loves order and would like 'a world where all would be silent and each thing in its place under the last dust' (p. 39), while Hamm accepts chaos in the hope that something will come out of it. Asked 'Why this farce day after day?', he answers, 'Routine. One never knows'. What they have in common is their perversity. Like the narrator in *Texts for Nothing*, they 'reason crooked', doing what they can, as Hamm remarks, to amuse themselves until the time for their extinction, or next dose of painkiller. Clov says: 'No-one that ever lived ever thought so crooked as we.' Hamm agrees: 'We do what we can' (p. 16). The theme of the play is death, and dying, and by making it a game they distance it. The characters have different reactions to the thought of death, Hamm delays the end by all the means in his power; Clov, on the other hand, sees death as an end of punishment.

Though they know that hope is illusory, for different reasons they cling to life. Hamm recalls a friend who turned away from the world. He alone had been spared, says Hamm, though he cannot emulate him. Clov has reached the stage where his chosen attitude to fate would be stoical indifference. He thinks that 'they' (the Gods?) might weary of punishing him and let him go, but feels 'too old and too far' to form new habits, so congratulates himself, 'Good, it'll never end, I'll never go' (though paradoxically when he does go, he says, he'll weep for happiness). Both he and Hamm seem 'doomed to hope unending' as the narrator says of Neary, in *Murphy*, using the same image (in which hope is symbolised by a flea). The discovery by Clov of a flea in their seemingly sterile world – an unwanted symbol of hope and continuity, perhaps – evokes echoes of Neary's query: 'Is there no flea that found at last, dies without issue? No key flea?' (*Murphy*,

p. 13). In *Endgame* there is comic wordplay about Clov's flea as to whether it is laying or lying doggo. If it is laying, as Hamm says, they are really in trouble for more fleas will be born, and it is not the 'key flea'. Thus, like Neary, they are doomed to hope on.

The expression of this hope, and what it is nourished by, are ideas, comical, bizarre, even fatuous. Tiring of enthusing about nature Hamm complains that she has forgotten them. Clov says hopefully that there's no more nature; and Hamm disagrees: 'No more nature – you exaggerate, we breathe, we change. We lose our hair, our teeth! Our bloom! Our ideals!' (p. 16), and Clov replies, 'Then she hasn't forgotten us.' They are amused by the contradiction that they decay, therefore they exist as part of nature. When Hamm turns from nature to ideas: 'To hell with the universe', and demands: 'An idea, have an idea (angrily) a bright idea.' Clov approves: 'Ah good' (p. 33). Generally these ideas take the form of games with words, quotations and jokes which provide the action of this almost motionless piece. Hamm becomes convinced that 'something is taking its course', and that they are maybe, in their stand against destruction, beginning to mean something. He makes a joke of it by parodying the reactions to their goings-on of a 'rational being', and puts on a 'rational' voice, saying pompously: 'Ah good, now I see what it is, yes now I understand what they're at' (p. 27). Clov demonstrates his own gift of repartee. Pointing his telescope at the audience he cries: 'I see . . . a multitude . . . in transports of joy' [Pause] 'That's what I call a magnifier' (p. 25). Clov feeds a line to Hamm: 'Do you believe in the life to come?', and Hamm answers, 'Mine was always that!' [Exit Clov] 'Got him that time' (p. 35). Or, when Clov asks what is keeping them there, Hamm answers: 'The dialogue'. Speaking of the demands of his retainers, Hamm borrows, and changes Marie Antoinette's alleged remark about the poor: 'It wasn't bread they wanted, it was crumpets' (p. 44). There is a music hall joke about a tailor who took longer to make a pair of trousers than the Almighty did to create the universe, but made them better, though the button-holes were 'ballocksed'. Clov says of a rat he has found and half-killed in his kitchen that, if he doesn't go back and finish it off, he'll die (p. 37). When Clov sees a child outside, another sign that this, maybe, is not a sterile world, Hamm says: 'Not an under-plot, I trust' (p. 49). A sub-plot would be a comic disaster, implying, as it does, the continuation of a play which otherwise seems to be petering out satisfactorily.

The location of *Endgame* has been described in several ways, for instance, the inside of a skull, or post atom bomb earth. An early MS version in fact locates it, in time and geographically, in such a devastated wasteland: 'dans la Picardie à quelque dix jours de marche bon train de Paris, détruite progressivement dans l'automne de 1914, le printemps de 1918, et l'automne suivant, dans des circonstances mystérieuses'.[3] Despite this uncompromisingly gloomy setting, Beckett's inborn dicacity is much in evidence, and there is a wide spectrum of humour in the piece, ranging from the arch or intellectual, to the *risus purus*, the defiant laugh at what is unhappy. This latter, in *Endgame*, reaches its apogee, and a fresh statement is made about the point of view of the author as far as humour is concerned. When Nagg sniggers at Hamm's misery, Nell rebukes him: 'One mustn't laugh at these things . . . Nothing is funnier than unhappiness, I grant you that. But – .' The 'but' shocks Nagg, and Nell continues: 'Yes, yes, it's the most comical thing in the world. And we laugh, we laugh, with a will, in the beginning. But it's always the same thing. Yes, it's like the funny story we have heard too often, we still find it funny, but we don't laugh any more' (p. 20). Beckett has said that this is the most important sentence in this play.[4] It heralds a viewpoint, finally taken in *How It Is*, when the contrasts of 'tears and laughter' are given their marching orders, for it is in *Endgame* that the funny story which is life is still found funny, but does not raise the usual laugh because the joke is too well known.

Beckett is beginning to discard humour as he discards material things. There is no more pap, sugar plums or coffins. *Endgame* looks forward to the late, reductionist works, in which the few props, including comedy, are reduced to even fewer. But the humour is not yet altogether discarded, because unhappiness can still inspire a joke. Even when the laugh is superfluous, Beckett's jests with language continue. When asked about the meaning of *Endgame*, he said his work is 'a matter of fundamental sounds (no joke intended) made as fully as possible', and that he would accept responsibility for nothing else. 'If people want to have headaches among the undertones, let them. And provide their own aspirin.'[5]

The 'message' of *Endgame* is positive. Speaking of his writing, Hamm says he has not got very far but 'I've got on with it a little all the same'. Clov says admiringly: 'Well I never! In spite of everything you were able to get on with it'. Hamm answers, 'Oh not very far you know, not very far, but nevertheless, better than nothing', to which Clov scathingly replies, 'Better than nothing! Is it possible?'. These are the voices of the author and his *alter ego*, and their contradictory perceptions of the value of the work. But the work is important in itself, whatever its merits or shortcomings. Beckett told the actors of the German version of *Endgame*: 'Hamm is saying no to nothingness',[6] and he puts into Hamm's mouth a positive injunction to the audience to get out of this limbo they share with him in the theatre, and get something done while there is yet time.

We know that Beckett saw *Endgame* as significant, because it expressed what he was trying to say. Dedicating it to his friend, Roger Blin, who staged the first production of *En Attendant Godot*, he wrote, 'it really has meaning, the others are only everyday'.[7] This Endgame has a close analogy to the phenomenon of existence in which you neither win nor lose, and which cannot be appraised until it is ended. Hamm holds off the end by refusing to declare himself beaten, although he knows that he will be beaten eventually. As he says: 'The end is the beginning and yet you go on!' (p. 44).

1956 was a fruitful year. In addition to *Fin de Partie*, in a notebook marked Eté 1956, Beckett produced first drafts of *All That Fall* (completed 1956), *Krapp's Last Tape* (completed 1958), *Comment C'est* (completed January 1960), and *Happy Days* (completed 1961).

All that Fall, written in English, was commissioned by the BBC and was published in 1957. In this short play for radio, set against an Irish village background, there is the typically Irish black humour and sense of the ridiculous found in plays by O'Casey or Synge. Many of its themes are echoes from past works, subjects for exasperated comedy; the longueurs of mundane existence, sexuality, the inhumanity of the conventional, disease, difficulties and incongruities of language and the unfairness of providence. It also demonstrates the real sympathy its flawed characters feel for each other, and their courage and tolerance in a difficult existence.

Bawdy or bizarre innuendos carry along this play in which the uncertainty of the human condition is made comic. In a world where it is 'suicide to be abroad', and to be at home is 'a lingering dissolution', the theme of the horrors of living at all is expanded by Mr Rooney, with a play on the words waxing, waning, in a witty and excruciating catalogue of the rites of housewifery: 'dusting, sweeping, airing, scrubbing, waxing, waning, washing, mangling, drying, mowing, clipping, raking, rolling, scuffling, shovelling, grinding, tearing, pounding, banging and slamming. And the brats, the happy little healthy little howling neighbours' brats. Of all this and much more the week-end, the Saturday intermission and then the day of rest, having given you some idea. But what must it be like on a working-day?' He compares this with the lesser horrors of being buried alive, if only from ten to five, in a 'silent backstreet, basement office, with its obliterated plate, rest-couch and velvet hangings', which has the consolations of 'a bottle of light pale ale' and a 'long ice-cold fillet of hake'.

Mrs Rooney's sexuality is lampooned; her obsession with horses' buttocks, her interest in the goings-on of the pigeons she calls Venus birds, her need for 'love': 'what normal woman needs affection?'. In tears over her long lost 'little Minnie' of forty years ago, she lewdly giggles, 'Oh glory . . . up! . . . up! . . .Ah! . . . I'm in!', as Mr Slocum, her old admirer, heaves her great weight into his car. She scandalises her husband, when they nearly fall into a ditch, by saying it would be 'like old times'. There is a reminder of the comedy of diseases in *Watt*. Mr Rooney complains of his wife's domination: the day they met he 'should have been in bed'. 'The day you proposed to me the doctors gave me up . . . The night you married me they came for me with the ambulance.' There is more black humour, when Mr Tyler praises the sky: 'What light. Ah in spite of all it is a blessed thing to be alive in such weather and out of hospital.' Mrs Rooney questions this sentiment: 'Alive?', and Mr Tyler answers, 'Well half alive shall we say?'. Mrs Rooney's reply is tart: 'Speak for yourself Mr Tyler. I am not half alive or anything approaching it'.

Descriptions are homely and funny. Mrs Rooney sees her shape as 'a big fat jelly slopped out of a bowl', and Mr Rooney sees her as a blancmange. When Miss Fitt affects not to see her, she enquires whether her cretonne dress is so becoming that she 'merges into the masonry'. There is comedy in the names of Slocum, Miss Fitt; etymological jokes, like the name for the men's lavatory, Fir, 'from Vir, viris', Mr Rooney thinks; literary jokes, Mr Rooney likens himself and Mrs Rooney to Dante's damned, with their faces 'arsy versy'. The vagaries of language are ridiculed. Mrs Rooney finds them 'excruciating'. Mr Rooney confesses he agrees, when he happens to overhear what he is saying. Mrs Rooney comforts him; language will be dead in time, 'just like our own poor dear Gaelic', and unfavourably compares this dying language with the baa of the lamb which 'has not changed since Arcady'.

The centrepiece of the play is the valedictory on a hen, run over by Mr Slocum, in the words of Mrs Rooney: 'What a death! One minute picking happy at the dung, on the road, in the sun, with now and then a dustbath, and then – bang! – all her troubles over. (Pause) all the laying and hatching. (Pause) Just one great squawk then . . . peace. (Pause) They would have slit her weasand in any case.' Here is a comment on the human lot as much as on the life of a hen, the shortness of their common existence and the likelihood of sudden death.

The chief joke, and backbone of the play, is in its title, a joke against God (Psalm 145): 'The Lord upholdeth all that fall and raise up all those that be bowed down', a text which, against a background of wind and rain, evokes wild laughter from the crippled Rooneys struggling, as Mrs Rooney says, to come home 'safe to haven'. Paradoxically, although the help of providence is not directly forthcoming, it is present in the aid they give each other, she acting as his eyes, he holding her up, the mutual help which sets the tone of the play. Ambivalent throughout, the play is a comment on the ambivalence of the human condition, and brings out the affirmative interaction between the characters in misfortune.

The next short play, *Krapp's Last Tape*, written in English for Patrick Magee in 1958, was published in the same year. Set in 'a late evening in the 1980s', the name in an early draft was 'Crapp' with a C.[8] Its hero is Beckett's perennially defiant loser, and it has the undertones of a personal swansong. Once again there is an attempt to sum up the argument of life versus art, and it displays a modification at each stage of the character's attitude to its polarities. The old Krapp is reviewing his own development. In an interview with Ronald Hayman in 1970 Beckett said, 'There is no resignation in Krapp even when he imagines that death is waiting for him. The character is eaten up by dreams. But without sentimentality. It's the end. He sees very clearly that he's through with his work, with love and with religion'. This short play (12 pages) is carefully structured. Technically a soliloquy, the tapes provide flashbacks to the desires and dreams of youth, the fading hopes of middle-age, the tragedy of old age, yet a return to dreams of youth. At each stage of his life, Krapp, the maturing Beckett hero, in looking back seeks inspiration for the present and future. As he says: 'old PMs are gruesome', but they are useful 'when embarking on a new retrospect'.

The play begins with pure farce. There is the theatrical effect of the clown garb, stage business with bananas including the classic music-hall or cinema slip on the discarded skin. These ploys, and the chink of bottle against glass, release tension and heighten the dramatic effect of the play's two diametrically opposed epiphanies; first, when the middle-period Krapp discovers that the dark he has tried to avoid is the source of his inspiration, and second, when old Krapp sees that the love, which he abandoned in order to write, is what he prefers, at this stage, to recall. It is significant that, to record this new standpoint, old Krapp puts on the recorder a 'virgin reel'.

In *Krapp's Last Tape*, Beckett has reached an important stage in his development as a writer, not only because it is a conscious 'farewell to love and work', but because the importance of love is acknowledged for the first time in the canon. Old Krapp listens to young Krapp giving up love for writing, yet at the same time recording memories of it 'against the day when my work will be done and no place left in my memory warm or cold'. He describes his younger self as 'a stupid bastard' and, listening to middle-aged Krapp gloating: 'Seventeen copies sold, of which eleven at trade price to circulating libraries beyond the seas. Getting known', he scoffs: 'One pound six and something. Eight I have no doubt.' Old Krapp, too, has his delusions. He thanks God he's 'finished with all that', but returns compulsively to the girl in the boat, and to the eyes of other girls; remembering the warmth of Bianca's, those of the unknown nursemaid, 'like crysolite', and declares: 'Everything there, everything on this old muckball, all the light and dark, and famine and feasting of all the ages! Reaffirming this he shouts, 'Yes! . . .' 'Let that go! Jesus!' It is a very positive moment and it is interesting that the girls have remained the same girls throughout the works. Middle-period Krapp's Bianca looks back to Belacqua's Alba; the girl in the boat to the Smeraldina of *More Pricks than Kicks*, and the earlier *Dream of Fair to Middling Women*, and maybe also to Murphy's Celia.

The contrasting light and dark tones of *Krapp's Last Tape* explore the tension between tragedy and comedy in the Pirandellian notion of one person's multiplicity of selves, through the device of Old Krapp looking back at his younger selves, particularly when he joins the middle-aged Krapp in a laugh at the youthful aspirations of the young Krapp. However, old Krapp, an excessive drinker, laughs alone at the young Krapp's resolution to cut down his drinking. The middle-aged Krapp is sententious on this subject, and quotes statistics: 'Seventeen hundred hours, out of the preceding eight thousand odd, consumed on licensed premises alone. More than 20 per cent, say 40 per cent of his waking life.' He is however more hesitant in commenting on young Krapp's plan for a 'less engrossing sex life', probably because it is during his time that the last illness of his father cost him such a 'flagging pursuit of happiness'. He detects something phoney in the younger Krapp's sneer at youth, thanking God it's over: 'False ring there', which he puts down to burgeoning obsession with writing, 'Shadows of the opus magnum' (p. 13). Old Krapp and middle-aged Krapp again share a hearty laugh at the young Krapp's naive 'yelp to Providence'. However, although there is real humour in middle-period Krapp's qualification 'or thereabouts' of his statement that he is intellectually 'on the crest of the wave', there is little real humour left in Old Krapp, though he can still laugh. And when the middle period Krapp asks what remains of 'all that misery' and answers: 'A girl in a shabby green coat, on a railway-station. No?', the 'no' indicates that there is a question whether that's all it was. It is certainly an important point for old Krapp, who becomes broody, and drinks three bottles in thirty seconds, breaks into a quavering childhood hymn and has a coughing fit, before resuming his listening position. This the highspot of the play, the reassessment of the argument between the various Krapps of what really was important in their experience, and the posing again of the question of the claims of life versus art; to which there is no answer for any of the Krapps. Old Krapp realises that it is a question which must be left open, and he dismisses himself and all the Krapps in a speech full of nostalgia:

Ah finish your booze now and get to your bed. Go on with this drivel in the morning. Or leave it at that. [Pause] Leave it at that. [Pause] Lie propped up in the dark – and wander. Be again in the dingle on a Christmas Eve, gathering holly, the red-berried. [Pause] Be again on Croghan on a Sunday morning, in the haze with the bitch, stop and listen to the bells. [Pause]

And so on. [Pause] Be again, be again. [Pause] All that old misery. [Pause] Once wasn't enough for you. [Pause] Lie down across her (p. 18).

And once again he poses the question, states the arguments, through the taped voice of middle-period Krapp, who speaks of the fire in him (which is dying in the old Krapp), and his goodbye to love. The old Krapp, motionless, still broods on that early love, and the old paradox.

The use of paradox is strong in *Krapp's Last Tape*, which is full of juxtapositions: the dark ('when I saw the whole thing. The vision at last') which was the source of light; the middle-aged Krapp, waiting for his mother to die, notes a nursemaid's 'incomparable bosom'; old Krapp, romantically recalling Effi Briest, and his own love, cutting to the present, and Fanny 'the old whore'. The paradox is especially poignant at the end, when the middle Krapp's voice gloats over the fire in him now, and old Krapp, listening to it, regrets the human relationships he exchanged for the 'fire', which he feels now is reduced to ashes. Despite this very real conflict, he does record his recent satisfaction with words: 'Happiest moment of the past half million'. Words have remained a constant source of reassurance for him, as well as an unwished-for compulsion. Paradoxically, although he is 'saying goodbye to work, love and religion', the writing is not yet finished, and he has not given up the idea of the possible existence of some superior power.

The manuscript notebook, marked Eté 1956, contains, in addition to the first version of *Krapp's Last Tape*, part of the first draft of *Happy Days*, the first complete version of which is dated 8 October 1960.[9] Nothing is absolute, and at the same time as Beckett was summing up his farewell to love and writing – in *Krapp's Last Tape* – his goodbye to laughter and tears in *How It Is*, he fired a Parthian shot at the follies of mankind in the ironically titled *Happy Days*. The alternative title, *A Low Comedy*, is the key to this play, which has nothing to do with the quest for the *risus purus*. It echoes the cruel sexual humour of *Watt*, and, like Watt, Winnie, in a wilderness she does not understand, 'makes a pillow of old words', and survives by imposing on her uncertain and baffling existence a series of rituals and habits, welcoming the intermittent bell because it gives a pattern to her day. Winnie's attitudes and language are a ludicrous mixture of the homely and the arty, and therein lies her success as a comic.

She and the shadowy Willie form another couple in the long line of Beckett couples. Together for no discernible reason, they react to each other with indelicacies, patronage and cruelties. Winnie, particularly, cannot bear to be alone, to 'prattle away with not a soul to hear' (p. 35), but so long as Willie exists she feels that 'something is being heard, I am not merely talking to myself . . . that is what enables me to go on, go on talking that is' (p. 32). Willie is her audience, to reflect her existence and prove that she exists. She says: 'I used to think that I would learn to talk alone . . . . By that I mean to myself, the wilderness . . . . But no . . . . No, no . . . . Ergo you are there.' She questions him, but does not value his answers: 'Do you think the world has lost its atmosphere, Willie? Do you Willie? (Pause) You have no opinion? (Pause) Well that is like you, you never had any opinion about anything' (p. 66). She tells him: 'It's a comfort to know you're there, but I'm tired of you.' (Pause) 'I'll leave you out, that's what I'll do' (p. 44). Willie has no significance for her, except as an ear to hear her. Her chief reassurance is her possessions, her parasol, or lipstick, even though they are gradually running out: 'Ah yes, things have a life, that is what I always say, *things* have a life' (p. 70).

Yet, despite her love of material objects, and the pretentiousness of her displays of learning, Beckett, with his usual ambivalence, brings out in Winnie the traits of human courage and humour. Immobile, she is glad that this increases her ability to talk: 'That is what I find so wonderful, my two lamps, when one goes out, the other burns brighter' (p. 48). Winnie is on her guard against acceptance and indolence: 'As the days go by, certain days go by, quite by, the bell goes, and little or nothing said, little or nothing done . . . . That is the danger. To be guarded against' (p. 48). So she rejoices that, although she cannot move, she is 'in tongue again' (p. 48). Like Molloy and Malone, better men than she is, but equally disadvantaged, Winnie is a story-teller. When all else fails, she says: 'There is my story of course . . . . A life . . . . (Smile) A long life' (p. 70). Winnie has the tenacity of all Beckett's deprived heroes, and the intention to tell her story is the mainspring of existence, and her main proof that she exists.

Concurrently with the cruelly observant *Happy Days*, in a return to the serious tone of *Krapp's Last Tape*, comes the masterly summing up of the writings so far: *How It Is*, originally entitled Pim, written in French between Summer 1956 and 6 January 1960.[10] A fragment appeared in *A Quarterly Review* (November, 1959, pp. 35–7) under the title 'L'Image', and an extract was published as 'From an Unabandoned Work' in *Evergreen Review* (Vol. IV no. 14, September–October 1960, pp. 58–65), before the publication of the French edition of *Comment C'est*, in 1961. The English translation, *How It Is*, by Beckett himself appeared in 1964. While writing it, Beckett said: 'the hole I have got myself into now is as "dumb of light" as the Fifth canto of Hell and by God no love',[11] yet *How It Is* has its felicities, and though the tone is sombre it is lightened by wit and wry comedy. In the first person, 'one voice here yes mine' (p. 58), it is, once again, the unique voice, which first broke through in *Texts for Nothing*, telling the narrator's own experience: 'We're talking of my life' (*Texts for Nothing*, p. 141), but it refers to everything ephemeral, not only his own 'fleeting joys and sorrows' but also 'empires that are born and die as though nothing has happened' (*How It Is*, p. 13).

How It Is is structured in three parts: before Pim, with Pim, after Pim. Beckett says it is a single eternity divided into three for the sake of clarity, though he adds the rider 'in trying to present in three parts or episodes which all things considered involves four, one is in danger of being incomplete' (p. 142). So it is a summing up of the first three quarters of the single eternity. It is written in 'natural order more or less' (p. 21), so it is not chronological and, indeed, past and present are confused as early as Part 1. He says his hold on things and language is uncertain, and he often falters, several times interjecting: 'something wrong there', but he declares it is true, 'I say it as I hear it every word always' (p. 24).

The story-teller, murmuring from a Dantean limbo, is tiring of his story-telling. Time is running out. He feels he is nearing the end of his journey and shows his relief: 'had I', he says, 'only the little finger to raise to be wafted straight to Abraham's bosom I'd tell him to stick it up' (p. 42). But he feels it is not yet time to raise the finger, and whimsically attempts one of his diversions: 'some reflections none the less while waiting for things to improve on the fragility of euphoria among the different orders of the animal kingdom beginning with the sponges' (p. 43).

The contradictions of *How It Is* mirror life: no more images, says the narrator, no more journeys. Yet it is full of images and journeys in time, though, as he says, the images are old ones: 'the kind I see sometimes in the mud' (p. 11); 'a few old images always the same' (p. 114). For Beckett, as for Proust, happiness is in the past but can be brought into the present, for the good moments of the past have become the good moments of the present. Memory keeps him going. When it fails he is 'mortal again'. Now that he is 'released from the wish to be less wretched the wish for a little beauty' (p. 13), he can recall the past in something approaching tranquillity. Laughter and tears are nearly finished. Conscientiously, he notes the deterioration of the sense of humour. Yet, for the first time, he says, he feels 'like someone who has tasted of love' (p. 14). 'I have that in my life this time'.

As in *Krapp's Last Tape*, there is nostalgia here for youth and spring, which are remembered in the mud as good moments, and felt again. He relives this experience and the memory is reinforcing: 'that must have lasted a good moment with that I have lasted a moment they must have been good moments' (p. 34). From the mud he sees again 'skies all sorts different sorts on land and sea blue of a sudden gold and green of the earth', and jibes at the 'weeping philosopher', who believed happiness could not be remembered in misery: 'that was a good moment saving the grace of Heraclitus the Obscure' (p. 38). As he retrieves 'the vast past near and far the old today' (p. 111); through memory, like Proust, he regains a sense of identity.

Now that he has almost repeated his life story, his pensum is nearly done: 'from it I learn from it I learnt what little remained learn what little remains' (p. 116), and he speaks ironically of this learning process, and his empirical approach to it, as 'refreshing alternations of history prophecy and the latest news whereby I learn in turn it's no doubt what keeps me young how it was my life we're still talking of my life' (p. 141). He wishes to be released from the pensum, and echoes Clov, 'it must and it's preferable only a third to go two-fifths and then part three and last', and, an echo from the *Unnamable*, 'one can't go on one goes on' (p. 96).

Reviewing his life 'through a spyglass, from the crib on' (p. 9), he marvels: 'the morals at the outset before things got out of hand' (p. 27). From this distance the past has glamour: 'abject abject ages', he says, 'each heroic seen from the next' (p. 10). Nostalgically he summons and captures memories: 'dear scraps recorded' (p. 28), and there are images of good moments as well as bad: 'to speak of happiness one hesitates', he says, 'but good moments yes I assure you', and, characteristically, he adds, 'and less good they must be expected' (p. 28). He recalls his mother, her hat, her severe expression as he knelt at her feet (p. 16). He recalls himself at sixteen, absurd, but with a girl 'under the sky of April or of May', a good moment relived, never to be forgotten: 'we are gone I stay there' (p. 35). He sees himself as Belacqua curled up asleep (p. 26), and says he would like to stay forever in the same place, 'never any other ambition'. He remembers when he 'hugged the wallow the midst of my brotherly likes', a play on words implying they did not like him, nor he their inhumanity: 'I screamed for help with once in a hundred some measure of success' (p. 41), and he humorously pictures one such occasion, when exceptionally the worse for drink 'at a small hour of the garbage-man' in his determination to leave the elevator he caught his foot 'twixt cage and landing and two hours later to the tick someone came running having summoned it in vain' (p. 41). If someone had not wanted the lift, he would never have been rescued. Comically paraphrasing Hamlet, he wishes for 'a little less of no matter what no matter how no matter when a little less of to be present past future and conditional of to be and not to be'. Again aping Hamlet, he asks is it a dream? and answers 'what a hope'.

All the old themes recur, there is still some life in the old ploys, and the narrator will not give up: 'when it's the last hope look for something else' (p. 117), 'find something else to last a little more' (p. 35), and questions can still fulfil this function. He now questions his own built-in scepticism: 'question if always good old question if always like that since the world world for me' (p. 47), but is still amused by life's contradictions. He feels the wish to laugh each time but, he says, the comedy is limited. Yet, as is his custom, he laughs at despair: 'saving your reverence I have the sufferings of all the ages I don't give a curse for it and howls of laughter in every cell' (p. 42).

The theme of couples, or the two sides of one persona, which runs through the works, is given a new image here. The narrator and Pim (or Bom or Bem) are one, tormentor and victim; it is his torture of Pim which produces the writings. Together they 'claw the armpit for the song carve the scriptions'. They are inseparable, and, when they feel this togetherness for an instant, it is such a great moment that it makes 'cruelty suffering so paltry so brief', because their interaction, and what comes out of it, proves they are alive and kicking: 'the voice extorted a few words life because of cry that's the proof good and deep no more is needed a little cry all is not dead' (p. 133). Self-torture makes him write, and we are asked 'kindly to consider' the proposition that 'while it is in our interest as tormentors to remain where we are as victims our urge is to move on'. For, he says, we are our own tormentors and our own victims, 'and of these two aspirations warring in each heart it would be normal for the latter to triumph if only narrowly' (p. 155). He adds: 'for as we have seen in the days that word again of journeys and abandons a most remarkable thing when you come to think of it only the victims journeyed' (p. 156).

It is the pain, and the journeying which may be productive. Our adverse reactions upon each other, our fragmentation and lack of understanding of ourselves, are the source of our questioning. Each one of us is at the same time Bom and Pim 'tormentor and tormented pedant and dunce wooer and wooed speechless and reafflicted with speech in the dark the mud' (p. 153). For we are all part of a great chain, linked 'in a vast imbrication of flesh without breach or fissure' (p. 153), reacting upon each other all along the line; all our joys and sorrows we 'extort and endure from one another' (p. 154). In this great chain of being – and he provides a Dantean image – we are 'a procession in a straight line with neither head nor tail in the dark the mud' (p. 135). We are told that he himself has experienced this endless process of existence: 'I have never quite fallen from my species and I made the journey.' He describes this never-ending passage of mankind: 'whose lot has been whose lot will be what your lot is' (p. 53), between life and death as an 'endless cortège' (p. 53), and quips: 'a procession what a comfort in adversity'.

Not only tears and laughter, but his old love and enemy, words, too are failing: 'we're still talking of words I have some still it would seem at my disposal at this period'. He will 'string them together make phrases more phrases' (p. 115). He tries to 'hear a few scraps two or three times a day and night' (p. 115). By this means, he is 'hanging on to humankind a thousand and one last shifts with emotions laughter and even tears to match soon dried in a word hanging on' (p. 103). On the other hand, the end of words are the end of life, he believes, and to be welcomed. His story-telling has kept him going, recording these 'little bits and scraps ill-heard ill-murmured and ill-recorded' which are, he says, 'my whole life a gibberish garbled six-fold' (p. 146).

And his story *was* his pensum, for he uses the same words in referring to the not-one-of-us who first devised our story, which is 'ill-inspired ill-told and so ancient so forgotten at each telling that ours may seem faithful that we murmur in the mud to him' (p. 151), and who listens, as we murmur it in the mud, this story of his own devising, our life, 'with its joys and sorrow journeys intimacies and abandons . . . we exhale it pretty much the same as the one he had devised'. For, he says, our murmurs ascend to where there is an ear and a mind to understand 'an ear to hear even ill these scraps of other scraps of an antique rigmarole' (p. 147), and this not-one-of-us, in listening to us, listens to himself (p. 150), for our voice is 'the voice of him who before listening to us murmur what we are tells us what we are as best he can' (p. 152).

Moreover this not-one-of-us prepared our existence, 'our sacks', and placed them 'here in position already like us all here in position at the inconceivable start of the caravan' (p. 148). We pick them up and carry them, as in a relay race, as far as we can. Our progress, he says, while admittedly laborious, is planned, our sacks allotted. When we drop them he believes our sacks are taken up by someone else, and, in some cases, progress is made. This image of the sack of existence is constant throughout this work. At the same time it is the source of joy and of sorrow: 'my sack sole variable my days my nights my seasons and my feasts it says Lent everlasting then of a sudden Hallowmas' (p. 18). His commitment to living, and to death, is in this sack, 'my sack thanks to my sack I keep dying in a dying age' (p. 18). And there is more to the sack than mere sustenance: it contains 'so many other things too so often imagined never named never could useful necessary beautiful to the feel' (p. 51). He repeats this thought later: 'no the truth is this sack I always said so this sack is something more than a larder than a pillow for the head than a friend to turn to a thing to embrace a surface to cover with kisses something far more' and he adds a testimonial to our sack of existence: 'I owed it this tribute' (p. 73).

Listening to us, and preparing our sacks, demands, he says, an intelligence, somewhere a love 'all along the track at the right places according as we need them' (p. 150) and, he says, given our number, it would be 'not unreasonable to attribute exceptional powers or else at his back assistants innumerable', because, we are asked to 'kindly consider that to hear and note one of our murmurs is to hear and note them all' (p. 150). And this intelligence and love are more than human, for they are 'that minimum of intelligence without which it were an ear like ours and that strange care for us not to be found among us and the wish and ability to note which we have not' (pp. 150–1). Who this being is he does not say; this time he has 'nothing to say almost nothing', about 'even God that old favourite my rain and shine brief allusions not infrequent in the tender years' (p. 77). The problem of God remains unsolved. He can't decide whether to curse God or bless him (p. 44), though later he curses God, blesses him, beseeches him (p. 53). He suggests there might be a solution, in 'a formulation that would eliminate him completely and so admit him to peace at last' (p. 157). We would then ourselves become responsible for our 'unqualifiable murmur' (p. 157), a relief, it is implied, both for us and for the not-one-of-us. And death is not to be feared but rather welcomed: 'no more journeys no more couples no more abandons ever again anywhere' (p. 26), he says: 'death if it comes that's all that dies'. He believes it is still possible at this late hour to conceive of another world 'where no one ever abandons anyone and no one ever waits for anyone and never two bodies touch' (p. 156).

Characteristically, in the last pages of *How It Is*, the narrator goes back on what he has said, even though he stated definitively that he has said it as it is: 'all these calculations yes the whole story from beginning to end yes completely false yes', however, he qualifies this: 'there was something yes' (p. 158). He remains certain of only four things. First, 'the mud and the dark are true' (p. 158). Secondly, there is 'only me alone in the mud the dark with my sack', and he drolly adds: 'I beg your pardon no no sack either no not even a sack with me no' (p. 159). Thirdly, all that remains for him are 'a few words yes a few scraps yes' (p. 160). And, fourthly, that he will die, which will bring positive relief.

Despite its obscurities, *How It Is* is Beckett's frankest work. In it the story-teller comes from behind the masks to hint at his own story, lowering the tension by seeing it in theatrical terms: 'life little scenes'. He is one with his *alter ego*, Pim: 'I too Pim my name Pim' (p. 66). But for him, he says, Pim would be a 'dumb limp lump flat forever in the mud' (p. 58). Their collaboration has not been easy: 'he floundered I floundered but little by little by little', but it has been productive: 'we had good moments they were good moments', which he downplays, 'drivel drivel no matter' (p. 68). Between them they composed his story: 'the childhood said to have been mine the difficulty of believing in it the feeling rather of having been born octogenarian' (p. 78). His papa had 'no idea but building trade', his mamma 'none either' (p. 86), there was the loved one dying whom he could not watch, 'how can one' (p. 85), looking at the furniture instead, 'love birth of love increase decrease death'; his isolation: 'never anyone never knew anyone always ran fled elsewhere some other place' (p. 86); his sense of failure in living; 'my life above what I did in my life above a little of everything tried everything then gave up' (p. 86).

He was, he says, 'not made for that farrago too complicated' (p. 86). He tried many lands, but returned 'home to native land to die in my twenties', though he did not die: 'iron constitution above in the light' (p. 93). He was 'a broken column in my thirties and still alive robust constitution what am I to do' (p. 94). However he sees humour in his short-comings: 'the dejections are me but I love them' (p. 43), and admits 'my mistakes are my life'. Yet there is a sense of achievement. If he has not succeeded in life, he has satisfied himself in his art, he has seen what was required of him, what he was fitted for: 'what is not beyond my powers known not to be beyond them song it is required therefore I sing' (p. 70), and he is glad that he has completed his task, has told his story, which he sums up: 'from sleep I come to sleep return between the two there is all the doing suffering failing bungling achieving' (p. 25). He believes he has said what was needed, put it into his writings: 'how it was the little there was I've said it I've been able I think so' (p. 108). Though his pensum is done, he has not finished writing. There is still part four, without which 'one is in danger of being incomplete' (p. 142). In *How It Is*, he feels at last that he has recited his task and has told it as it was, as it is.

Yet 'the end of laughter and tears' is not the end of the story. In 'Part 4, without which one is in danger of being incomplete', the voice in limbo continues to ruminate, and the war with words continues. There are still words left after *How It Is*: 'I have some still it would seem at my disposal'. These later works, which Beckett has described as residua, echo his old preoccupation with human foibles, continue to try to make sense of existence, and, latterly, and more important, explore ways of expressing formlessness in fantastic imagery and fragmented and reduced language.

Conclusion

In half a century of writing Beckett has mirrored the endless process of creation, in which individual existence is transitory, and so, to our short view, seems chaos. 'Nothing changes', he says, 'except tiny changes due to the customary cycle of birth, life, death' (*Molloy*, p. 55). Nevertheless, these decades cover a period of significant transition. From the 1930s to the 1980s many changes have taken place in the sociological and literary spheres. Beckett himself has played an important part in this transition, and his work has influenced later writers, among them Iris Murdoch and Harold Pinter, as well as the ideas of a wider, very varied audience.

Elusive and enigmatic, he speaks for an age which sees life as a series of existential moments. Throughout the works his impressionistic picture of life's antinomies has influenced new and changing universal perceptions. As he has said, 'up to the present century, art has imposed form on chaos, but in these times confusion invades our experience at every moment, therefore it must be allowed in . . . to find a form that accommodates the mess, that is the task of the artist now.'[1] True to this idea, he presents us with material as hard to assimilate as what it is about.

This unconventional style of writing makes the reader's task difficult. It is hard not to be tempted to 'wring its neck in order to stuff it into a contemporary pigeon-hole' (*Our Exagmination* (1929)), and vital to avoid this temptation, because it cannot be applied to a work of art, which is *sui generis*. To quote Beckett: 'The chartered accountants take the thing to pieces and put them together again. They enjoy it. The artist takes it to pieces and makes a new thing, new things. He must.'[2] Out of this compulsion to make a new thing comes a new form of literature.

The works, from the beginning, bear witness not only to Beckett's inborn dicacity, but, more seriously, to the way in which the humour throughout is related to the search for a philosophy for what he sees as the mainly painful experience of existence. In his definition of the stages of humour which correspond to 'successive excoriations of the understanding', Beckett has provided a guide. The early stages – 'the ethical' laugh at what is not good, 'the intellectual' at what is not true – imply criticism, and Beckett's early works are critical of God and existence. His youthful iconoclasm and comic genius are given full rein in *More Pricks than Kicks* (1934) and *Murphy* (1936).

After this, the tone is less high-spirited. *Watt*, written in wartime (1943–5) becomes blacker and more cruel, but is extravagantly funny on the sexual level. After *Watt*, with the change to writing in French, there is new inspiration for games with language. In *Mercier and Camier* (1946), there is the beginning of a move towards the *risus purus*, 'the laugh laughing at what is unhappy', and an equivalent philosophical point of view. The dark and the light of existence are examined with black irony and 'a sense of proportion' is recommended. Mercier and Camier are the prototypes of Vladimir and Estragon and share their humour and philosophy.

In *Molloy* and its sequel, *Malone Dies* (1947–8), the narrator is tiring, but, to continue writing, he deploys pastimes, comic sexual adventures, moments of euphoria on a bicycle, digressions and jokes to stave off *accidia*. In *Waiting for Godot* (1948), the theatre provides relief from the psyche-probing, and existence is seen as tragi-comedy; not tragedy because these heroes will not accept defeat, as tragic heroes would, and make use of all the digressions, jokes and pastimes they can, to delay any decision about their tedious existence. For them, laughing at what is unhappy is a defence against finality. The *Unnamable* (1949–50), blind and paralysed, but bitterly witty, is equally determined not to give in. In the *Texts for Nothing* (1950–2), defeat very nearly overtakes the writing and produces the famous 'impasse', but the narrator can still jest: 'there's nothing like breathing your last to put new life in you' (p. 10). A laugh, he says, distances the horrors 'especially of oneself, and everything becomes a game' (p. 29). The writing – the search for himself – must go on; he has to make sure he has 'left no stone unturned' before 'reporting myself missing and giving up' (p. 36).

In *Endgame* (1956) Hamm, a reincarnation of the Unnamable, like him, delays the end of the game. He is also related to Vladimir and Estragon, so there are still games with the audience, but in this play the *risus purus* is achieved. The 'funny story' of life, though still funny, does not raise a laugh. Beckett is discarding humour as he discards things, and in the reductionist later works he will cut down on words, too. But before that there is the earthy humour of *All that Fall* (1956), the knockabout, as well as the 'farewell to work and love', of *Krapp's Last Tape*, the black humour at the expense of Winnie, in *Happy Days*, all of which were conceived in 1956.

In *How It Is*, also begun in 1956 and published in 1961, the author finds his form, and himself, at last: 'one voice here yes mine' (p. 58). It is the breathless, unpunctuated, summing up of all that has been written already. A certain calm has been attained, and a 'deterioration of the sense of humour fewer tears too' is noted. The past, its joys and pains, can be recalled almost tranquilly. The pains had their uses, it is decided, because they have inspired the work. Now the pensum is done, the task recited, and the 'greater', 'inner', 'finer' level of understanding has been reached, where the conflict between laughter and tears can be ignored, though the writing continues.

In 'Part 4', in the 1960s, human failings continue to capture Beckett's attention. In *Play* (1963) for instance, a middle-class trio – husband, wife, mistress – reflect impassively, in their urns in limbo, on their situation. In *Come and Go* (1965) middle-aged women gossip about 'the old days'.

Continuing the attempt to make sense of existence is treated, for example, in *Not I* (1972) in which a mouth (contrived by lighting) disembodied, reflects with laughter and screams on a lifetime from birth to old age, or *Company* (1981) in which a dying character asks for one moment more of memories of the past: 'One last. Grace to breathe that void. Know happiness.'

The important part of the continuing work after *How It Is*, however, is devoted to finding a way to express what Beckett sees as the formlessness of existence, culminating in *Ill Seen, Ill Said* (1982), which notes the failure, yet importance of words: 'See now more words too. A few drops mishaphazard. Then strangury. To say the least' (p. 52). Or in *Worstward Ho* (1983), about words again, 'just enough still to joy' (p. 29) which are what keeps the writer going. And there is still humour in the words 'mishaphazard' or 'Worstward Ho'.

Notes and References

1. Beckett's Literary Antecedents and Some Philosophers

1. Vivian Mercier, *The Irish Comic Tradition* (Oxford University Press, 1962).
2. Review of *More Pricks than Kicks*, *The Listener*, 4 July 1934, p. 42.
3. 'The Roots of Samuel Beckett', *The Listener*, 17 December 1964.
4. John Fletcher, *Samuel Beckett's Art* (New York: Barnes & Noble, 1967) p. 94.
5. Samuel Johnson, Preface, *Shakespeare*, ed. W. Raleigh (London: Macmillan, 1908) pp. 15–16.
6. Deirdre Bair, *Samuel Beckett* (London: Jonathan Cape, 1978) p. 275. There are some 300 letters extant from Samuel Beckett to Tom MacGreevy, from the 1930s up to MacGreevy's death in 1967. His literary executors allowed Deirdre Bair to see them, and quotations from these letters appear in her *Samuel Beckett*, 1978.
7. L.-F. Céline, *Mort à credit* (Paris: Editions Denoël & Steele, 1936) p. 518.
8. Interview with Claude Bonnefoy, 'Dernier adieu à sa jeunesse', *Arts*, 833, 3–9 August 1961, p. 5.
9. Letter to Milton Hindu, *Texas Quarterly* v, No. 4, 1962, p. 32.
10. Letter to E. Pollet, August, 1933, *L'Herne*, No. 3, p. 100.
11. Ruby Cohn, *The Comic Gamut* (New Brunswick: Rutgers University Press, 1962) p. 99.
12. Ruby Cohn, *Back to Beckett* (Princeton, NJ: Princeton University Press, 1973) p. 14.
13. John Montague, Review of *James Joyce* by Richard Ellmann, *Guardian*, 21 October 1982.
14. Letter to P. Magee, 15 December 1975. Quoted Bair, p. 639.
15. John Pilling, *Samuel Beckett* (London: Routledge & Kegan Paul, 1976) p. 123.
16. 'Dante . . . Bruno. Vico . .' in Joyce, *Our Exagmination . . . of Work in Progress* (London: Faber, 1972).
17. *The Novelist as Philosopher*, ed. J. Cruickshank (Oxford University Press, 1962) p. 3.
18. Address on the presentation of an Honorary D.Litt. Degree at Trinity College Dublin, 1959, translated by A. J. Leventhal and quoted in Bair, p. 504.
19. Ludovic Janvier, *Beckett par Lui-même* (Paris: Editions du Seuil, 1969) Chronologie.
20. Jean Anouilh, 'Godot ou le sketch des Pensées de Pascal traité par les Fratellini', *Arts-Spectacles* 394, 16 January 1953, p. 3.
21. Letter to T. MacGreevy, 21 September 1937, quoted Bair, p. 261.
22. Henri Bergson, *Le Rire. Essai sur la signification du Comique* (Geneva, 1945).

23. Tom F. Driver, interview with Samuel Beckett in *Le Monde*, quoted John Pilling, *Samuel Beckett* (London: Routledge & Kegan Paul, 1976) p. 129.

2. Beckett and the Theatre

1. Alec Reid, *All I Can Manage, More Than I Could* (Dublin: Dolmen Press, 1968).
2. Letter to Barney Rosset, Grove Press, 11 February 1955. An important primary source of information about Beckett's view of his works is the collection of letters he wrote to Barney Rosset, Grove Press, in the Grove Press Collection, George Arents Research Library, Syracuse University, New York, to whom I am indebted for photocopies.
3. Ruby Cohn, 'Inexhaustible Beckett', *An Introduction to Samuel Beckett. A Collection of Criticism* (New York: McGraw-Hill, 1975) p. 10.
4. Letter to T. MacGreevy, 13 March 1948, quoted Bair, p. 374.
5. Letter to Jean Reavey, 6 August 1962, quoted Bair, p. 550.
6. J. Fletcher and J. Spurling, Introduction, *Beckett. A Study of his Plays* (London: Eyre Methuen, 1970).
7. Preface. *Breasts of Tiresias.* Quoted in *Modern French Plays*, eds Michael Benedikt and George E. Wellwarth (London: Faber, 1964).
8. W. B. Yeats, *Autobiographies* (New York: 1958) pp. 233–4.
9. John Fletcher and John Spurling, *Beckett. A Study of his Plays* (Harmondsworth: Penguin, 1978) p. 41.
10. 'Aliéner l'Acteur', 12 May 1947. Quoted in Martin Esslin, *Artaud* (Harmondsworth: Penguin, 1976) p. 76.
11. Antonin Artaud, *The Theatre and its Double*, trans. M. C. Richards (New York: Grove Press, 1958) p. 42.
12. Ronald Hayman, *Theatre and Antitheatre* (London: Heinemann, 1979).
13. 'La Peinture des Van Velde, ou le monde en pantalon', *Cahiers d'Art*, Nos 20 and 21 (Paris, 1945–6).
14. Antonin Artaud, *The Theatre and its Double*, trans. M. C. Richards (New York: Grove Press, 1958).
15. 'Manifesto of Surrealism', *transition*, March 1932, pp. 148–9.
16. 'Recent Irish Poetry', *Bookman* 86, 1934, p. 235. Under the pseudonym Andrew Belis.
17. *Times Literary Supplement*, 23 October 1937, p. 786.
18. *Dream of Fair to Middling Women* (unpublished novel) (1932).
19. Walter Starkie, *Luigi Pirandello* (London: Dent, 1926) p. 181.
20. Ibid., p. 248.
21. Ibid., p. 251.
22. Luigi Pirandello, *L'Humorismo* (Florence, 1920) p. 179. Quoted in J. L. Styan, *The Dark Comedy* (Cambridge: Cambridge University Press, 1968) p. 47.
23. Interview with Tom F. Driver, 'Beckett by the Madeleine', *Columbia University Forum* IV, Summer 1961, pp. 21–5.
24. Luigi Pirandello, *On Humor.* Introduced, translated and annotated by

Antonio Illiano and Daniel P. Testa (University of North Carolina Press: 1960) p. 35.
25. W. B. Yeats, *Plays and Controversies* (1923) pp. 143, 154.
26. Review of Sean O'Casey, *Windfalls*. Quoted in Bair, p. 183.
27. *The Times*, 26 November 1929.
28. Sean O'Casey, *Modern Judgements*, ed. R. Ayling (London, 1969) p. 91.
29. Vivian Mercier, *The Irish Comic Tradition* (Oxford University Press, 1962) p. 248.
30. Eric Elliot, 'Anatomy of Motion Picture Art', in Rachel Low, *The History of British Film, 1919–1929* (London: Allen & Unwin, 1971) p. 42.
31. Ernest Betts, 'Heraclitus, or the Future of Films', in Rachel Low, *The History of British Film, 1919–1929* (London: Allen & Unwin, 1971) pp. 14–16.

3. The 'Impasse' of Language

1. Colin Duckworth, *En Attendant Godot* (London: Harrap, 1966). Introduction, p. xliii.
2. A. J. Leventhal, 'The Beckett Hero' in Martin Esslin (ed.) *Samuel Beckett. A Collection of Critical Essays* (New Jersey: Prentice-Hall, 1965) p. 46.
3. I. A. Richards, *Principles of Literary Criticism* (London: Routledge, 1965) p. xii.
4. Quoted in Bair, p. 557.
5. W. B. Yeats, *Explorations* (London: Macmillan, 1962) p. 255.
6. *The Drunken Boat*. Thirty-six poems by Arthur Rimbaud, with English translations by Brian Hill (London: Rupert Hart-Davis, 1952). Introduction, p. 9.
7. Lawrence Harvey, *Samuel Beckett, Poet and Critic* (Princeton, NJ: Princeton University Press, 1970) p. 72.
8. Richard L. Admussen, *The Samuel Beckett Manuscripts. A Study* (Boston: G. K. Hall, 1979) p. 57.
9. Collection of Samuel Beckett's Letters to Barney Rosset, Grove Press, in George Arents Research Library, Syracuse University, New York.
10. *transition*, March 1932, pp. 148–9.

4. The Early Works (1930–45)

1. In Reading University Library.
2. Reviewed in *Trinity College Dublin Weekly*, November 1929.
3. Ruby Cohn, *Samuel Beckett: the Comic Gamut* (New Brunswick: Rutgers University Press, 1962).
4. MS in private hands (see Admussen, p. 102).
5. In Dartmouth College Library, New Hampshire (see Admussen, p. 105).

6. Letter of 8 April 1956. In George Arents Research Library, Syracuse University, New York.
7. Letter to Tom MacGreevy, 13 May 1933, quoted in Bair, p. 165.
8. Quoted in Bair, p. 229.
9. Letter to G. Reavey, 13 November 1936, quoted in Bair, p. 243.
10. To Colin Duckworth, quoted in *En Attendant Godot*: A Critical Edition (London: Harrap, 1966) p. xvi.
11. Letter to Sighle Kennedy, quoted in *Murphy's Bed* (1971) p. 300.
12. Letter to G. Reavey, 28 September 1935, quoted in Bair, p. 243.
13. Letter of 14 May 1947, quoted in Bair, p. 364.
14. He appears again in *Mercier and Camier*.

5. First Steps in French

1. To John Fletcher. Quoted in *The Novels of Samuel Beckett* (London: Chatto & Windus, 1970) p. 102.
2. To Patrick Magee, 26 March 1976, quoted in Bair, p. 403.
3. Admussen, p. 67.
4. To John Fletcher, Ruby Cohn, Deirdre Bair and others, quoted in Bair, p. 361.
5. Letter to G. Reavey, 14 May 1947, quoted in Bair, p. 359.
6. Letter to G. Reavey, 8 July 1948, quoted in Bair, p. 389.
7. Letter to G. Reavey, 15 August 1947, quoted in Bair, p. 367.

6. The Trilogy: 'Prime, Death, Limbo'

1. He told Deirdre Bair, July 1973, quoted in Bair, p. 403.
2. Letter of 14 January 1948, quoted in Bair, p. 372.
3. To John Fletcher, quoted in *The Novels of Samuel Beckett* (London: Chatto & Windus, 1970) p. 102.
4. Letter of 13 March 1948, quoted in Bair, p. 374.

7. *Waiting for Godot*

1. Quoted by John Fletcher in his 'Afterword' and 'Notes' to *Waiting for Godot* (London: Faber, 1971) p. 108.
2. Letter to Barney Rosset, Grove Press, 14 December 1953. Beckett said: 'Repetition has its function in the sense that it reinforces the repetitive text. The symbols are variety and the whole affair is monotony.'
3. Letter to Roger Blin. 9 January 1953, quoted in Bair, p. 428.

8. 'Impasse'

1. Admussen, p. 54.
2. See Admussen, p. 110.

9. 'The laugh of laughs laughing at what is unhappy'

1. Ruby Cohn, *Back to Beckett* (Princeton NJ: Princeton University Press, 1973) p. 154.
2. Roger Blin. Quoted in Bair, p. 483.
3. Admussen, p. 13.
4. Quoted in Bair, p. 468.
5. Alan Schneider, 'Beckett's letters on *Endgame*', *Village Voice*, 19 December 1957, p. 185.
6. Ruby Cohn, *Back to Beckett* (Princeton NJ: Princeton University Press, 1973) p. 152.
7. Letter to Roger Blin with typescript of *Endgame*, undated. Quoted in Bair, p. 479.
8. Admussen, p. 61.
9. Admussen, p. 55.
10. Admussen, p. 32.
11. Letter to Jake Schwartz, 5 November 1959, quoted in Bair, p. 512.

Conclusion

1. Tom F. Driver, 'Beckett by the Madeleine', *Columbia University Forum* IV, Summer 1961, pp. 21–5.
2. Samuel Beckett, Review of Jack B. Yeats, *The Amaranthers* (London: Heinemann, 1936) in *Dublin Magazine*, July–September, 1936, p. 80.

Bibliography

PRIMARY

The works of SAMUEL BECKETT used here are listed in chronological order of composition:

Le Concentrisme. Paper read to the Modern Language Society of Trinity College, Dublin, c. 1928. (In Reading University Library.)
'Dante . . . Bruno. Vico . . Joyce', in Our Exagmination round his Factification for Incamination of work in Progress (London: Faber, 1972).
'Whoroscope' (Paris: Hours Press, 1930).
Review of Le Kid, written in French with Georges Pelorson, and performed by the Modern Language Society of Trinity College, Dublin, at Peacock Theatre, Dublin. TCD: A College Miscellany, 26 February 1931.
A Dream of Fair to Middling Women. Unpublished novel, 1932. MS in Reading University Library.
'Manifesto of Surrealism', transition, March 1932, pp. 148–9 (with Thomas MacGreevy and others).
'Recent Irish Poetry', review of the work of young poets, Bookman, 86 (1934) p. 235. Under the pseudonym of Andrew Belis.
Review of Jack B. Yeats, The Amaranthers, Dublin Magazine, July–September 1936, p. 80.
'La Peinture des Van Velde ou le monde en pantalon', Cahiers d'Art 20–21 (1945–6) pp. 349–54 and 356.
Proust and Three Dialogues with Georges Duthuit (London: Calder & Boyars, 1965).
More Pricks than Kicks (London: Calder & Boyars, 1970).
Murphy (London: John Calder, 1977).
Watt (London: John Calder, 1976).
First Love (London: Calder and Boyars, 1973).
Four Novellas ('The End', 'The Expelled', 'First Love', 'The Calmative') (London: John Calder, 1977).
Mercier and Camier (London: Calder & Boyars, 1974).
Eleuthéria (unpublished play). Typescript in Reading University Library.
Molloy (London: John Calder, 1976).
Malone Dies (London: Calder & Boyars, 1975).
Waiting for Godot (London: Faber & Faber, 1965).
The Unnamable (London: Calder & Boyars, 1975).
Texts for Nothing (London: Calder & Boyars, 1974).
'From an Abandoned Work', in Six Residua (London: John Calder, 1978).
Abandoned play ('Ernest and Alice'). Typescript lent by Reading University Library.
Endgame (London: Faber & Faber, 1964).

136

All that Fall (London: Faber & Faber, 1965).
Krapp's Last Tape (London: Faber & Faber, 1965).
Happy Days (London: Faber & Faber, 1978).
How It Is (London: Calder & Boyars, 1972).
Le Bateau Ivre: Drunken Boat, trans. S. Beckett with Introduction by James Knowlson and F. Leakey (Reading: Whiteknights Press, 1970).
Collected Poems (London: Calder & Boyars, 1977).
Nouvelles et Textes pour Rien (Paris: Editions de Minuit, 1954).
That Time (London: Faber, 1976).

SECONDARY

ADMUSSEN, RICHARD L., *The Samuel Beckett Manuscripts. A Study* (Boston, Mass., G. K. Hall, 1979).
ALLSOP, KENNETH, *The Angry Decade. A survey of the cultural revolt of the 1950s* (New York: British Book Centre, 1958).
ANOUILH, JEAN, 'Godot ou le sketch des Pensées de Pascal traité par les Fratellini', *Arts-Spectacles*, 400 (27 February–5 March 1953).
ANSCOMBE, ELIZABETH and GEACH, PETER THOMAS (eds), *René Descartes. Philosophical Writings* (London: Nelson, 1970).
ARTAUD, ANTONIN, *The Theatre and Its Double*, trans. M. C. Richards (New York: Grove Press, 1958).
AYLING, R. (ed.), *Sean O'Casey, Modern Judgements* (London, 1969).
BAIR, DEIRDRE, *Samuel Beckett* (London: Jonathan Cape, 1978).
BENEDIKT, MICHAEL and WELLWARTH, GEORGE (eds), *Modern French Plays* (London: Faber, 1964).
BERGSON, HENRI, *Le Rire. Essai sur la signification du comique* (Geneva, 1945).
BISHOP, THOMAS, *Pirandello and the French Theatre* (New York: University Press, 1960).
BONNEFOY, CLAUDE, 'Céline. Dernier adieu à sa jeunesse', *Arts* 833, 3–9 August 1961, 5.
BRANDEIS, IRMA, *The Ladder of Vision. A Study of Images in Dante's Comedy* (London: Chatto & Windus, 1960).
BULLITT, JOHN M., *Jonathan Swift and the Anatomy of Satire* (Cambridge, Mass.: Harvard University Press, 1953).
CELINE, L.-F., Letter to Milton Hindu, *Texas Quarterly*, 4, 1962.
CELINE, L.-F., Letter to E. Pollet, August 1933, *L'Herne* No. 3, p. 100.
CELINE, L.-F., *Voyage au bout de la nuit* (Paris: Editions Denoël & Steele, 1932).
CELINE, L.-F., *Mort à credit* (Paris: Editions Denoël & Steele, 1936).
COHN, RUBY, 'The Comedy of Samuel Beckett: Something Old, Something New', *Yale French Studies*, 23, Summer 1959, pp. 11–17.
COHN, RUBY, 'Still Novel', *Yale French Studies* 24, Fall 1959, pp. 48–53.
COHN, RUBY, A note on Beckett, Dante and Geulincx, *Comparative Literature*, 12, 1960.
COHN, RUBY, *Samuel Beckett. The Comic Gamut* (New Brunswick, NJ: Rutgers University Press, 1962).

COHN, RUBY (ed.), *Casebook on Waiting for Godot* (New York: Grove Press, 1967).

COHN, RUBY, *Back to Beckett* (Princeton University Press, 1973).

COHN, RUBY, 'Inexhaustible Beckett', in: *An Introduction to Samuel Beckett. A collection of criticism* (New York: McGraw-Hill, 1975).

COHN, RUBY, *Just Play. Beckett's Theatre* (Princeton University Press, 1980).

CROSS. W. L., *Life and Times of Laurence Sterne* (New Haven: Yale University Press, 1965).

CRUICKSHANK, J. (ed.), *The Novelist as Philosopher. Studies in French Fiction 1935–1960* (Oxford University Press, 1962).

DRIVER, TOM F., 'Rebuke to Nihilism', *Christian Century* LXXVII, 2 March 1960, pp. 256–7.

DRIVER, TOM F., 'Beckett by the Madeleine', *Columbia University Forum* IV, Summer, 1961, pp. 21–5.

DUCKWORTH, COLIN, *En Attendant Godot* (London: Harrap, 1966).

DUCKWORTH, G. E., *The Nature of Roman Comedy* (Princeton University Press, 1967).

ESSLIN, MARTIN (ed.), *Samuel Beckett. A Collection of Critical Essays* (New Jersey: Prentice-Hall, 1965).

ESSLIN, MARTIN, 'Samuel Beckett', in *The Novelist as Philosopher, Studies in French Fiction 1935–60*, ed. John Cruickshank (New York: Oxford University Press, 1962).

ESSLIN, MARTIN, *Artaud* (Harmondsworth: Penguin, 1976).

FEDERMAN, R. and FLETCHER, J., *Samuel Beckett. His works and his critics* (University of California Press, 1970).

FITCH, B. T., 'Bardamu dans sa nuit à lui', *Bulletin des Jeunes Romanistes*, 8 December 1963.

FLETCHER, JOHN, 'Samuel Beckett and Jonathan Swift. vers une étude comparée', *Littératures* X, Annales publiées par la Faculté des Lettres de Toulouse XI, No. 1, 1962, pp. 81–117.

FLETCHER, JOHN, 'Beckett and the Fictional Tradition', *Caliban* 2, Annales publiées par la Faculté des Lettres de Toulouse (1965).

FLETCHER, JOHN, *Samuel Beckett's Art* (New York: Barnes & Noble, 1967).

FLETCHER, JOHN, *The Novels of Samuel Beckett* (London: Chatto & Windus, 1970).

FLETCHER, JOHN, 'Afterword' and 'Notes' to *Waiting for Godot* (London: Faber, 1971).

FLETCHER, JOHN and SPURLING, JOHN, *Beckett. A Study of His Plays* (London: Eyre Methuen, 1970).

FURBANK, P. N., 'Beckett's Purgatory', *Encounter* XXII (June 1964) pp. 69–70, 72.

HARVEY, LAWRENCE, *Samuel Beckett. Poet and Critic* (Princeton University Press, 1970).

HAYMAN, RONALD, *Samuel Beckett* (London: Heinemann, 1968).

HAYMAN, RONALD, Interview with Samuel Beckett, *The Times*, 15 April 1970.

HAYMAN, RONALD, *Theatre and Antitheatre* (London, 1979).

HESLA, DAVID, *The Shape of Chaos* (University of Minneapolis Press, 1971).

JANVIER, LUDOVIC, *Pour Samuel Beckett* (Paris: Editions de Minuit, 1966).

JANVIER, LUDOVIC, *Beckett par lui-même* (Paris: Editions du Seuil, 1969).

JOHNSON, SAMUEL, Preface to *Shakespeare* (ed. W. Raleigh) (London: Macmillan, 1908).

JOHNSON, SAMUEL, *Diaries*, Yale Works, 1.78 and vi.

JOHNSON, SAMUEL, *Life*, ii.

JOHNSON, SAMUEL, *Adventurer*, ii.

JOHNSON, SAMUEL, *A Poem, and the Vanity of Human Wishes*. With introductory essay by T. S. Eliot, 1930.

JOHNSON, SAMUEL, *Rambler*.

JOYCE, JAMES, *Letters*.

KAISER, W., *Praisers of Folly* (London: Gollancz, 1964).

KENNEDY, SIGHLE, *Murphy's Bed* (Lewisburg, Pa.: Bucknell University Press, 1971).

KENNER, HUGH, 'Samuel Beckett v. Fiction', *National Review*, vi, 11 October 1958.

KENNER, HUGH, 'The Absurdity of Fiction', *The Griffin*, viii, November 1959.

KENNER, HUGH, *The Stoic Comedians* (London: W. H. Allen, 1964).

KENNER, HUGH, *Samuel Beckett. A Critical Study* (University of California Press, 1968).

KENNER, HUGH, *Readers' Guide to Samuel Beckett* (London: Thames & Hudson, 1973).

KNOWLSON, JAMES, 'Afterword' to *Happy Days* (London: Thames & Hudson, 1978).

KNOWLSON, JAMES, *Samuel Beckett: An Exhibition* (London: Turret Books, 1971).

KOTT, JAN, 'Ce monde tragique et grotesque', *Critiques de motre Temps*, ed. D. Nores (Paris, 1971).

KOTT, JAN, '*King Lear* or Endgame' (1964) in: *Shakespeare. King Lear. A Casebook*. ed. Frank Kermode (London: Methuen, 1969).

LEVENTHAL, A. J., 'The Thirties', in: *Beckett at Sixty. A Festschrift* (London: Calder & Boyars, 1969).

LOW, RACHEL, *The History of British Film 1918–1929* (London: Allen & Unwin, 1971).

MacNEICE, LOUIS, *Varieties of Parable* (Cambridge University Press, 1965).

MERCIER, VIVIAN, *The Irish Comic Tradition* (Oxford University Press, 1962).

MERCIER, VIVIAN, *Beckett/Beckett* (Oxford University Press, 1979).

MONTAGUE, JOHN, Review of Richard Ellmann's *James Joyce*, *The Guardian*, 21 October 1982.

MUIR, EDWIN, Review of *More Pricks than Kicks*, *The Listener*, 4 July 1934, p. 42.

MURDOCH, IRIS, 'Against Dryness', *Encounter* xvi (January 1961) pp. 16–21.

OREGLIA, G., *The Commedia dell'Arte*, trans. L. F. Edwards (London: Methuen, 1968).

OSTROVSKY, ERIKA, *Céline and his Vision* (University of London Press, 1967).

PASCAL, BLAISE, *Pensées* (London: Dent, 1954).

PILLING, JOHN, *Samuel Beckett* (London: Routledge & Kegan Paul, 1976).

PINGAUD, BERNARD, 'Importance de Samuel Beckett à sa date', in *Critiques de notre Temps*, ed. D. Nores (Paris, 1971).

PIRANDELLO, LUIGI, *L'Humorismo* (Florence, 1920).

PIRANDELLO, LUIGI, *On Humor*. Introduced, translated and annotated by Antonio Iliano and Daniel P. Testa (University of North Carolina Press, 1960).

REID, ALEC, *All I can Manage, More than I could* (Dublin: Dolmen Press, 1968).

RICHARDS, I. A., *Principles of Literary Criticism* (London: Routledge, 1965).

RICKS, CHRISTOPHER, 'The roots of Samuel Beckett', *The Listener*, LXXII, 17 December 1964.

RIMBAUD, ARTHUR, *The Drunken Brat. Thirty-Six Poems with English translations by Brian Hill* (London: Rupert Hart-Davis, 1952).

ROBBE-GRILLET,ALAIN, 'The case for the new novel', *New Statesman* LXI, 17 February 1961.

SARTRE, J.-P. *Existentialism and Human Emotions* (New York: Citadel Press, 1971) (Part of which: 'Existentialism and Humanism' was published in 1945).

SCHNEIDER, ALAN. 'Beckett's letters on *Endgame*', *Village Voice Reader*, New York: 19 March 1958.

SCOTT, N. A. *Modern Literature and the Religious Frontier* (New York: 1958).

SHAW, G. B., *Our Exagminatia*.

SHAW, G. B. Review of Sean O'Casey's Plays. *The Times*, 26 November 1929.

SIDNEY, PHILIP, *In Defence of Poesie* (Oxford University Press, 1966).

STARKIE, WALTER, *Luigi Pirandello* (London: Dent, 1926).

STEINER, GEORGE, *The Death of Tragedy* (New York: 1961).

STEDMOND, JOHN L. *The Comic Art of Laurence Sterne* (Toronto University Press, 1967).

STYAN, J. L. *The Dark Comedy, The Development of Modern Comic Tragedy* (Cambridge University Press, 1968).

SYPHER, WYLIE, Appendix to: *Comedy, An Essay on Comedy*, George Meredith, and *Laughter*, Henri Bergson (New York: 1956).

WARD, D. *Jonathan Swift: An Introductory Essay* (London: Methuen, 1973).

WELSFORD, ENID, *The Fool. The social and literary history* (London: 1935).

WILLIAMSON, HENRY, *A Dream of Fair Women* (London: 1924).

WILSON KNIGHT, G., '*King Lear* and the Comedy of the Grotesque' (1930), in *Shakespeare, King Lear. A Casebook*, ed. Frank Kermode (London: 1969).

WORTH, KATHARINE J., *Revolutions in Modern English Drama* (London: G. Bell, 1972).

WORTH, KATHERINE J., *Beckett the Shape-Changer* (London: 1975).
WORTH, KATHERINE J., *The Irish Drama of Europe from Yeats to Beckett* (London: Athlone Press, 1973).
YEATS, W. B., *Plays and Controversies* (London: Macmillan, 1923).
YEATS, W. B., *Autobiographies* (London: Macmillan, 1926).
YEATS, W. B., *Explorations* (London: Macmillan, 1962).

Index

142